EUTHANASIA

Moral and Pastoral Perspectives

RICHARD M. GULA, S.S.

PAULIST PRESS

Portions of this volume were previously published in a slightly different form as "Euthanasia and Assisted Suicide: Positioning the Debate," © 1994 by the Catholic Health Association of the United States.

Cover Design by John Murello of Valley Stream, N.Y.

The publisher gratefully acknowledges use of: excerpts from Chaim Potok, MY NAME IS ASHER LEV (New York: Ballantine Books, 1972), p. 150, used with permission; excerpts from SHADOWLANDS by William Nicholson, copyright © 1990 by William Nicholson, used by permission of Dutton Signet, a division of Penguin Books USA Inc.

Library of Congress Cataloging-in-Publication Data

Gula, Richard M.
    Euthanasia : moral and pastoral perspective / Richard M. Gula.
      p. cm.
    ISBN 0-8091-3539-6 (pbk.)
    1. Euthanasia—Moral and ethical aspects. 2. Euthanasia—Religious aspects—Catholic Church. I. Title.
R726.G847   1995   94-34075
179'.7—dc20   CIP

Published by Paulist Press
997 Macarthur Boulevard
Mahwah, NJ 07430

Printed and bound in the
United States of America

CONTENTS

INTRODUCTION

R.I.P. is not yet the epitaph we can write for the efforts to legalize euthanasia and physician-assisted suicide. The 54 to 46 percent defeats of both Washington's 1991 "aid-in-dying" initiative (Prop 119) and California's 1992 "Death with Dignity Act" (Prop 161) has not laid euthanasia and physician-assisted suicide legislation to rest. Death's habit of arriving accompanied by the fear of enduring pain, of being trapped by machines without control, of losing bodily integrity and personal dignity, of costing a great deal financially and emotionally, along with other factors, lends strength to the movement to secure an all-purpose silver bullet by legalizing euthanasia and physician-assisted suicide. Efforts in this direction are not going to disappear any time soon. Connecticut, Florida, Maine, Michigan, New Hampshire, Oregon, and California again have these issues on the docket. If one state legalizes it, others are likely to follow.

Even though the legislative efforts have failed, the popular support for legalizing euthanasia remains strong. Poll after poll in the last twenty years has shown a steady increase of Americans (age and religious affiliation notwithstanding) agreeing that doctors should be allowed by law to end a terminal patient's life if the patient requests it.[1]

The initiative battles have been fought largely on pragmatic grounds. For instance, the key strategy of the campaigns against the initiatives in Washington and California was to argue from the "lack of safeguards." Television spots

1

tugging at the heart were another major strategy for both sides and were harder to refute. Using testimonials, proponents had terminally ill cancer patients push the right to choose "a humane and dignified death." Opponents had cancer survivors testify that life is worth fighting for.

In fact, the debate about euthanasia and physician-assisted suicide is more a debate about competing and conflicting moral visions and values than anything else. This book tries to identify the main features of the visions and values shaping the debate, especially those upheld by the Catholic moral tradition.

Those who have followed the arguments in the professional literature for and against euthanasia and physician-assisted suicide will not find anything new here. This overview does not intend to move the argument in new directions. The purpose here is to make a resource available to those who have not been able to follow the professional literature, but who still want to be informed about the major positions being taken on this issue. Its focus is primarily on how the Catholic religious and moral tradition positions itself in the debate, and what kind of pastoral response to the euthanasia movement it can support.

The argument from Catholic religious convictions and moral tradition presented here does not appeal to everyone. It presumes faith and a certain depth of commitment to the Catholic moral tradition. To provide a rationally persuasive case against euthanasia in the public arena, the Catholic Church does not always make its religious perspectives explicit. Rather, we often translate the concepts and values of our tradition into the language and arguments of the common moral ethos. As in any translation, something gets lost. In this case, we lose our distinctive religious reasons and motivation. One aim of this book is to light up the main lines of the religious argument of the Catholic Church. Thus, it focuses on the religious perspective from which the Catholic moral tradition derives its opposition to euthanasia and physician-assisted suicide.

The first chapter clarifies the object of the debate, since a misunderstanding of what is being advocated or opposed only brings more heat than light to the issues. Once we clarify the object of debate, then we can examine the vision and values at stake. The next three chapters frame the vision and values at stake within the scope of *autonomy*, the scope of the *prohibition against killing*, and the scope of *beneficence*. The final chapter tries to "walk the talk," as it were, by sketching a pastoral response to the euthanasia movement. It will identify the virtues, personal and corporate, which witness to the kind of moral and spiritual life we need to live if our arguments against euthanasia are to be credible.

I am grateful to the Catholic Health Association for their encouragement to do this project and for their permission to adapt materials from my earlier work, *Euthanasia and Assissted Suicide: Positioning the Debate*,[2] and the document, *Care of the Dying: A Catholic Perspective*,[3] of the task force on the Catholic Tradition Speaks to Suffering and Dying. Both of these latter projects were commissioned by CHA to provide educational resources for their member facilities. This new project has been adapted from those sources and expanded with a pastoral focus that will serve a wider audience.

1. THE DEBATE

What the Debate Is Not About

The easiest way to skew this debate is to see it as a "pulling-the-plug" issue. It is not. What Richard McCormick wisely observed in the context of distinguishing killing from allowing to die can be said of the object of the euthanasia debate: "One way to soften resistance to the unacceptable is to confuse it with the acceptable."[1] Forgoing useless or disproportionately burdensome treatment (which is what we generally mean by "pulling the plug") is not the same as euthanasia or assisted suicide. Standard medical, moral, and legal practices allow the competent patient, or surrogate of an incompetent patient, to weigh according to the patient's values the benefits and burdens of being treated, and then to select from alternative treatments or to refuse treatment altogether. The traditional Catholic medical-moral principle of the ordinary/extraordinary means standard supports such practice as the morally proper way to care for the dying. To refuse treatment which is useless or disproportionately burdensome (i.e., extraordinary) is the morally appropriate forgoing of treatment. It is *not* euthanasia nor assisted suicide.

What the Debate Is About

The debate *is* about voluntary active euthanasia and physician-assisted suicide. Voluntary active euthanasia means a deliberate intervention, by someone other than the person whose life is at stake, solely intended to end the life of the competent, terminally ill patient who makes a fully voluntary and persistent request for aid in dying. A common way to think about euthanasia is that of having a physician give a lethal injection to the patient who wants to die. "Mercy killing" is commonly used in place of euthanasia to emphasize that such an act is solely intended as an act of kindness.

In a physician-assisted suicide, a physician helps to bring on the death of the patient by providing the means to do it, or by giving the necessary information on how to do it, but the patient performs the lethal act on himself or herself. Dr. Jack Kevorkian has popularized this form of killing. The typical procedure of assisted suicide is the patient taking a lethal dose of poison (by swallowing pills, by taking an injection, or by inhaling a gas, for example) requested of and then prescribed by the physician for that purpose. In this case, as in euthanasia, both the physician and patient play morally responsible roles in bringing about death. Physician-assisted suicide is not morally different from euthanasia and need not be distinguished for purposes of understanding the moral vision and values at stake in the present debate.

To summarize, the debate is about whether it is ever acceptable morally, and so ought to be permissible legally, for a physician to take the life of a competent, terminally ill patient *who requests it*, or for a physician to assist the competent, terminally ill patient to take his or her own life. The debate is *not yet* about involuntary euthanasia—an intervention intended to kill a person who is incapable of making a request to die (such as an infant, a young child, a mentally retarded person, or a comatose patient). Seeking moral and public support for involuntary euthanasia may be the next phase. The debate also is *not* about whether it is ever permissible to withhold or withdraw ("pull the plug") useless or disproportionately burdensome treatment. However, as Corrine Bayley reports from her experience in the debate over Proposition 161 in California, the fact that the legislative initiative was not about refusing treatment was a fine point lost on many people. Many saw the initiative as an opportunity to secure assurance that they will be able to take matters into their own hands when it comes to the way they die.[2]

The Arguments

The basic line of argument supporting euthanasia and physician-assisted suicide can be summarized as follows. On the grounds of respect for autonomy, human persons should have the right to control their living and dying, and so they should be able to end their lives when they wish to terminate needless suffering. Physicians, as agents of the patient's best interests, should assist either by directly killing the patient or by assisting the patient in suicide. Euthanasia and assisted suicide are beneficent acts of relieving human suffering.

The main line of the religious argument against euthanasia and assisted suicide is as follows. Human persons are stewards of creation and so have only limited dominion and thus limited freedom over their lives. Human life is a "trust," and not a personal "possession" over which we can assume full control. The sanctity of human life is conferred by God and requires nurturance and protection. Taking life is not a human right, but a divine prerogative. Human suffering, while not a value in itself, can have meaning when lived in faith and so not diminish human dignity.

2. AUTONOMY

Autonomy is the centerpiece in the moral defense of euthanasia. The prevailing interpretation of autonomy is that of ethical liberalism, which attributes a supreme value to the individual's freedom and rights. When defenders of euthanasia appeal to autonomy, they mean that each person has a right to control his or her body and life, including the end of it, and so ought to be given the freedom to exercise this right. Thus we hear the familiar appeal to the so-called "right to die."[1]

For advocates of euthanasia, autonomy is based on the conviction that human dignity lies in being the bearer of basic rights and freedoms, especially the freedom to make of ourselves what we want to be by deciding according to our own values and plans. Anything that stands in the way of "free choice" assaults personal dignity. One of their major contentions is that we will have a better life, and a better death, to the extent that we have control. They seek through euthanasia to assure us of that last definitive step in gaining full self-determination so that we can die as we choose.

In this view, physicians are expected to follow the demands of the patient not only to end treatment upon request, but even to kill the patient, because the right to choose must be respected. In fact, the "right to choose" is the primary value. Absolutizing this right, as ethical liberalism does, makes "free choice" the sole right-making characteristic of an act. Other values (such as one's responsibilities to and for others) that ought to inform the exercise of autonomy do not have much influence. For example, H. Tristram Englehardt, Jr., a strong advocate for the liberal interpretation of autonomy, has argued that what makes killing immoral is that we do not have the patient's permission to do it, not that we have no such sovereignty over life.[2]

Autonomy is limited, according to ethical liberalism, only by the obligation to respect others' freedom to choose and to follow their own plans, or to fulfill commitments still outstanding, or not to cause harm to others. To challenge or to interfere with an autonomous person, especially when his or her actions are not harming anyone else, is considered not only to be bad social form but also disrespect of human dignity.

In health care, autonomy has a prominent place as the guiding principle for treating the patient as a person with values, goals, and limits. But this same freedom which preserves the patient's right to refuse treatment is now being extended by advocates of euthanasia to include choosing death and the means to achieve it, even to the extent of eliciting the assistance of another if necessary and desired.[3] Euthanasia, if legalized, would be the ultimate civil liberty, since it would secure the freedom to determine and to control our own death.

The dominant value upheld by the principle of autonomy is self-determination. It is such a supreme value because it means that you and I can live according to our own conceptions of the good life. I am ultimately responsible for my life, and you are responsible for yours. The human dignity attached to the freedom of self-determination demands respect for the freedom to choose and to control not only life but also how and when we die. The "right to die" and "death with dignity" in this view may be translated as something like the following: "It's my body; it's my freedom; it's my life; it's my death. Let me have control." Absolutizing autonomy in this way makes "death with dignity" mean that each of us should be able to determine at what time, in what way, and by whose hand we will die. While no one doubts that self-determination is an important value, the question in the euthanasia debate is, "How far does autonomy extend?"

Many people believe that autonomy, and the value of self-determination, extends to choosing the time and manner of one's death. Exit polls after the defeat of Proposition 161 in California showed that 65 percent of those who supported the initiative did so on the basis of their belief in the "right to die."[4] This is a clear indication that the value of self-determination is in the bloodstream of the American people. The public seems committed to not interfering in an autonomous choice. As a society, we have a great tolerance for letting people do their own thing, even if it means seeking assistance in suicide.[5]

Perhaps we can understand the desire to extend autonomy to include the choice for euthanasia when we consider the larger context of dying in America and the view many have of the way they will die. Most deaths today occur in a health-care facility. There, machines are used to prolong life so that patients become extensions of the machines. They no longer feel themselves to be self-determining persons who have control over their lives. This was confirmed by the experience of the members of the campaign to defeat Prop 119 in Washington. The coalition learned that "people have only one perception of how they die—hooked up to tubes and machines in an intensive care unit with no control."[6] Turning to euthanasia is an understandable response to a death that is difficult to make peaceful because dying is caught in technological traps.

Euthanasia looks like the best way to avoid the tyranny of technology, the fear of being trapped, and the loss of independence and dignity. Daniel Callahan has correlated the increasing support for legalizing euthanasia with the increasing fear many people have of being trapped in unacceptable conditions of dependency and disability brought about by medicine's power to prolong dying.[7] The right to refuse life-sustaining treatment is not enough to allay those fears. Some people can adjust to the disabilities and the dependence that some forms of life-sustaining treatment bring. They are the ones who can find meaning and value in living a new way while dying. Others cannot. They find their impairments too great to make life worth living any longer. They are the ones likely to seek euthanasia if it were legally available. They justify it morally on the basis of the value of preserving their dignity by exercising their "right to choose" and so determine the manner and time of their deaths.

AUTONOMY: RELIGIOUS PERSPECTIVE

A counter-argument to justifying euthanasia on the basis of autonomy can be made from the religious beliefs and moral philosophy of the Catholic moral tradition. The argument appeals to a combination of the principles of divine sovereignty and human stewardship, and the social ethics principle of the common good. These principles shape an argument against justifying euthanasia on the basis of autonomy.

The Principles of Sovereignty and Stewardship

According to Christian belief, we live in a world of grace. The first story of creation (Gen 1–2:4) tells us, in a symbolic way, that when humans appeared on the sixth day, all the rest of creation was already in place. This is a way of telling us that everything comes to us as a gift from a totally free act of a gracious God. The story is pervaded with a sense of man and woman being trusted with gifts, the gifts of creation and of one another. These gifts are to be cherished and shared, not hoarded and abused. Life is such a gift, a precious one at that.

Novelist Chaim Potok, in *My Name Is Asher Lev*, has written well about the fundamental attitude of reverence toward life as a gift from God. In the following scene, Asher Lev recalls a childhood memory of the way his father once spoke of the preciousness of life when they came upon a bird lying dead against the curb of their house:

> "Is it dead, Papa?" I was six and could not bring myself to look at it.
> "Yes," I heard him say in a sad and distant way.
> "Why did it die?"
> "Everything that lives must die."
> "Everything?"
> "Yes."
> "You, too, Papa? And Mama?"
> "Yes."
> "And me?"
> "Yes," he said. Then he added in Yiddish, "But may it be only after you live a long and good life, my Asher."
> I couldn't grasp it. I forced myself to look at the bird. Everything alive would one day be as still as that bird?
> "Why?" I asked.
> "That's the way the Ribbono Shel Olom made His world, Asher."
> "Why?"
> "So life would be precious, Asher. Something that is yours forever is never precious."
> "I'm frightened, Papa."
> "Come. We'll go home and have our Shabbos meal and sing zemiros to the Ribbono Shel Olom."[8]

Human life is God's gift to us and our responsibility. Our belief in God as Creator and sustainer of life engenders an attitude of reverence for life as a precious creation of God for which we are responsible. This attitude of reverence is enshrined in the principle of the sanctity of life. The limits of our responsibility for life is enshrined in the principles of sovereignty and stewardship. Together these principles temper destructive intrusions into life and demand good reasons for any action that would take life (e.g., killing in self-defense). Human life, as God's gift and our responsibility, is not properly reverenced by putting others at the disposal of our whims, ambitions, or desires to serve some utilitarian end.

The principles of sovereignty and stewardship assert that God has absolute dominion over creation, and we share in it only as limited creatures (Gen 2:7). Even with limited dominion, our human glory is that we can transcend some of the limits of being creature by cooperating with God who continues to act in history by opening new possibilities for human well-being. While we can transcend some of our limits, we must consent to others.

The second story of creation expresses in an imaginative way the limits that come with being created human and not being the sovereign Creator (Gen 2:15–17). The fundamental distinction between Creator and created sets limits on our freedom and the scope of our stewardship. No one can ever claim total mastery over creation, including one's life. As the story goes, the first man ("earth creature" is the better translation) was placed in the garden of Eden but forbidden to eat from the fruit of the tree of the knowledge of good and evil. To eat of that tree would impart a mastery of life and an autonomy inappropriate for being human.

This story asserts a fundamental conviction of biblical faith that from the very beginning human freedom over life was limited. Thus, our religious beliefs in God's dominion and human stewardship already limit the extent of our freedom.[9] Pope John Paul II affirmed as much in *Veritatis*

Splendor where he draws on this very passage from Genesis to assert:

> The man ["earth creature"] is certainly free, inasmuch as he can understand and accept God's commands. And he possesses an extremely far-reaching freedom, since he can eat "of every tree of the garden." But his freedom is not unlimited: it must halt before the "tree of the knowledge of good and evil," for it is called to accept the moral law given by God (*VS*, no. 35).

The principles of sovereignty and stewardship have found their way into the euthanasia debates through those who have followed the third argument of St. Thomas against suicide: God alone, as Creator, has sovereignty over life and death. The end of human life is not subject to a person's free judgment (II-II, q. 64, a.5 and a.5, ad.3). Humans have only a right to the *use* of human life as a "trust" or a "gift" from God, but not to dominion over it as a personal "possession." Thus, our responsibility for life is one of stewardship, not ownership. Our freedom does not extend to absolute dominion. Absolute dominion is an exclusively divine prerogative.

The contemporary moral theologian, Bernard Haring, has argued against human freedom extending to include the direct intervention in the dying process on the basis of sovereignty and the limits of human stewardship. According to Haring, we exercise our freedom in death by accepting ourselves as creatures of God and by admitting to our powerlessness in the face of death. Our freedom does not extend to bringing about death at the time and under the conditions we stipulate.[10]

The Principle of the Common Good

The social nature of being human also limits our freedom. The prevailing interpretation of autonomy is directed toward cultivating self-realization apart from any concern of how our personal desires and striving contribute to the good of society as a whole. Within this ethos of individualism, no one can tell anyone else what is good for him or her, or for us. Individualism is skeptical of there being any good beyond that which any single person takes to be good in his or her experience.

However, the social nature of being human challenges such a view. Everyone is located in social relationships. That is a given. We are born into social networks, nurtured by them, fulfilled in them, and even frustrated by them. We can't escape them. So if we put too much emphasis on autonomy, we fail to realize that any changes in our social relationships can change the way we develop. In this light, we can appreciate the Catholic moral tradition's insistence that the communal aspect of life must be structured to support the dignity of each person. Thus, any expressions of personal freedom must be assessed with its social implications. This holds for the way we die, too. For the way we die is shaped by and, in turn, shapes our relationships with others. Therefore, euthanasia must be scrutinized in light of communal values and commitments.

The principle of the common good provides an ethical framework for making that assessment. This principle, though an integral part of the Catholic tradition of social justice, is still not familiar to many, and it is not an easy one to grasp. Since it has not been given the popular attention other aspects of the Catholic moral tradition have received, such as aspects of Catholic sexual ethics, many Catholics would not be able to name it as influencing their thinking. Yet the spirit of this principle flows in our bloodstream still. For example, a story circulating during the debates on California's Prop 161 (The Death with Dignity Act) shows the Catholic instinct for what this principle aims to protect even if Catholics do not recognize it as such.

As the story goes, a distinguished professional with a seriously crippling disease took his life with the help of some friends. He had asked his wife, a Catholic, to help him, but she couldn't. She recalled that when he was very ill, he would say, "I just can't handle this—you've got to help me." But she would say, "No, not tonight. I can't deal with it tonight." Then she would go out to the road and cry. She was going to vote against Prop 161 because she felt it lacked safeguards and would lower our general inhibition against taking life. But she did not feel her being a Catholic made a difference in this matter. As she explained, "I don't think it's my Catholicism talking. I think it's what I know about the society we live in and how easily it devalues what ought to be treasured."

Actually, her Catholicism was talking. She just didn't recognize it. The part of Catholicism that subconsciously inspired her criticism of society, and made her fearful of what we would do to human dignity if we legalized killing by euthanasia, is enshrined in the principle of the common good. This principle directs us to assess the implications for society as a whole of any changes we make in our social practice. This principle has not been made explicit in the public debates on euthanasia, yet its perspective is the theoretical framework for the "no safeguards" strategy of the campaigns against the initiatives in Washington and California.

Charles Dougherty, Director of the Creighton Center for Health Policy and Ethics, has made a compelling argument against euthanasia from the perspective of the common good.[11] His argument is based on the conviction that there is a good for society as a whole beyond a good for each person. We call this good "the common good." While it respects and serves the interests of individual persons, the common good ultimately upholds the collective good as more important than the good of any one individual. It believes that the individual will flourish only insofar as society as a whole flourishes. To seek the common good, then, is to seek those actions and policies that would contribute to the total well-being of persons and the community.

Because it is a collective good, protecting it may frustrate some individuals from attaining specific goods for themselves. Dougherty illustrates this point with the example of traffic lights.[12] The common good demands that we regulate the flow of traffic in our cities. Thus, we install traffic lights. These structure our social relationships in ways that frustrate an individual citizen's desire to get around as quickly as he or she might like, but the structure serves everyone's interests and is necessary for public order. Yet, the common good cannot be limited to the public order or even to shared material goods. It must be taken in a holistic sense to cover all aspects of who we are as human persons.

Dougherty shows that one of the reasons that the common good has not been able to get a foothold in the euthanasia debate is that the diversity in our society makes it difficult for us to appreciate that there can be some good that is of value to us as a whole, irrespective of our differences.[13] As long as we continue to envision society as a loose association of diverse individuals bound together by self-interest, then we will continue to miss the value of the common good. It envisions society as an interdependent community where individual good is bound up with the good of the whole. Thus, there can be no sharp distinction between private and public spheres, since we are interdependent persons. What we do in pursuing personal goals bears on the well-being of the whole society. A commitment to the common good forces us to ask whether there are some things that we want for ourselves but which we ought not to pursue so that the good of the whole might better be served. In short, this principle holds in perpetual tension the relation between satisfying personal goods and contributing to the good of society.

Another reason why it is difficult for this principle to get a foothold in the debate is that it demands that we shift the way we analyze euthanasia. We must move away from the individual perspective which analyzes it as a private issue and move toward the societal perspective which analyzes it as a social issue. If we treat dying as a strictly personal and private affair, we ignore the social forces shaping the way we die. The common good reminds us that the way Aunt Mary dies is important not only to her, but to society at large.

Daniel Callahan has argued along these lines to claim that permitting euthanasia would be "self-determination run amok."[14] It cannot properly be classified, he claims, as a private matter of self-determination or as an autonomous act of managing one's private affairs. Euthanasia is a social decision. It involves the one to be killed, the one doing the killing, and it requires a complying society to make it acceptable. Therefore, euthanasia must be assessed in its social dimensions. Precisely for this reason, the appeal to autonomy to justify euthanasia for one individual does not adequately account for the social dimensions of that individual act nor the impact that sanctioning euthanasia as a practice will have on the common good. Any discussion of euthanasia, then, ought *not* to be limited to what helps or hinders individual well-being. Rather, it must reach beyond the individual to include the impact that individual acts of euthanasia have on community welfare. Therefore, autonomy must be understood within the limits of the social responsibilities for the common good.

Another reason why the common good argument hasn't taken hold is that it is countercultural. We are immersed in ethical liberalism which exalts individual rights and self-interests over the common good. Ethical liberalism likes to resolve conflicts and formulate policy in the direction of maximizing individual liberty. It tends not to look beyond satisfying private goals. From the perspective of ethical liberalism, the morally right and wrong become tied to one's own free choice. Whether or not one's interests and means of satisfying them contribute to the well-being of society is not its issue. The real issue for ethical liberalism is what contributes to self-realization. It is *not* how our interests will affect the good of the whole.

The principle of the common good calls us to imagine the potential impact introducing euthanasia will have on caring for the dying and on our general attitude toward life and the taking of life. One possible impact of introducing euthanasia into our present health-care delivery system, where costs are high and access uneven, is that patients, families, and physicians may turn to it as a way to be more cost-effective. Euthanasia will certainly save money and free space, physical and emotional, for other acute cases.

In addition, we are enamored of the quick-fix of technology. Our heavy dependence on technology to fix our health problems is tied to our tendency to look always for the easiest solution. We use technology to avoid the more difficult changes in lifestyle. Ready access to euthanasia may be our way out of finding better ways to relieve pain, to support the impaired, or to engage the imagination to find ways to live through suffering. Access to euthanasia also might erode the efforts that are made to secure the right to refuse unwanted treatment, or it might threaten the relationship of trust between physician and patient, or even undermine the character of medicine as committed to caring in all instances and to healing what can be cured.

Furthermore, those who live with impairments and draw on social supports financially, or in any other way, can easily be forced to justify their existence now that they have a way out and can relieve society of the burden of their care. Similarly, euthanasia as a policy can threaten to establish social standards of acceptable life. The vulnerable, those with serious dementia or depression and who cannot speak for themselves or defend their values, may be especially at risk of being killed. Overall, the practice of euthanasia threatens to weaken the general prohibition against killing in society and so we end up valuing life less.

CONCLUSION

These are only some aspects of the Catholic vision and values which make up the religious perspective of the debate on euthanasia from within the scope of autonomy. Euthanasia perpetuates the illusion that we can control everything, that we can be masters of nature and of death. By drawing on its religious beliefs about God's sovereignty and the limited scope of responsible stewardship for life, as well as its social ethical tradition of advocating for the common good, the Catholic tradition recognizes limits to autonomy and so challenges its support for euthanasia.

3. THE PROHIBITION AGAINST KILLING

The distinction between killing and allowing to die is at the heart of the euthanasia debate. Killing is any action or omission intended to cause death. Allowing to die is withholding or withdrawing useless or disproportionately burdensome treatment so that nature may run its course, i.e., so that the fatal condition may overtake a person. The Catholic tradition holds to a moral difference between, on the one hand, withholding treatment from a dying patient when nothing more can be done to reverse significantly the progressive deterioration of life; and, on the other hand, intervening to put the patient to death. Only the latter is prohibited.

The Catholic tradition does not look on withholding or withdrawing useless or disproportionately burdensome treatment as an act of killing. From a moral point of view, withholding treatment is evaluated the same way as withdrawing treatment. The benefit/burden criterion applies in either case. That is to say, if the benefits of the treatment are not or will not be proportionate to the burdens the patient will have to bear as a result of the treatment, then the treatment can be withdrawn if already started or withheld if not yet begun. Even though withholding and withdrawing treatment are not morally different, withdrawing treatment may be the more difficult emotionally because we are less likely to stop something once begun than we are not to start it at all.

KILLING VS. ALLOWING TO DIE

The significance of the distinction between killing and allowing to die and its importance for the euthanasia debate cannot be underestimated. The stance one takes on whether killing and allowing to die are morally different greatly affects the stance one takes in the euthanasia debate.

No Moral Difference

One extreme position holds to no moral difference between killing and allowing to die. This is the position represented by the Hemlock Society and philosophers such as Jonathan Glover, Peter Singer, Michael Tooley, Marvin Kohl, Helga Kuhse, James Rachels, and others. For James Rachels, for example, the distinction is simply a descriptive difference in actions to terminate life.[1] Since death is the outcome in either case, there is no moral difference between killing and allowing to die. So, once we decide not to prolong Uncle Ralph's dying, whether we actively intervene to cause his death or passively allow him to die makes no moral difference. While other factors (such as Uncle Ralph's preference) may intervene to make one means morally different from the other, the fact that his death comes by actively killing him or by allowing him to die is not *itself* a reason to think one is morally better than the other. According to Rachels, since there is no moral difference between killing and allowing to die, our present acceptance of allowing to die ought to be extended to active killing, when such killing would be more merciful.

Qualified Difference

Others will hold that the distinction does have moral significance, but that it dissolves at a certain point in the process of dying. For example, one of the leading Protestant medical ethicians, the late Paul Ramsey, opposed euthanasia on the basis that it is incompatible with the demand of covenantal fidelity that we owe one another and its imperative never to abandon care. His ethics accepts the moral difference between killing and allowing to die, but he recognized that some patients, such as those in irreversible coma or intractable pain, may move beyond the reach of being given care and comfort and receiving it. At that point, the distinction between killing and allowing to die dissolves. Then Ramsey would allow for an exception to the general rule against euthanasia. Ramsey does not fear a weakening of the general rule prohibiting euthanasia as long as the exceptions to it are limited to those patients who are truly beyond the reach of human care and comfort.[2]

Robert Veatch lists five different arguments for holding to a difference between killing and allowing to die. For him, killing and allowing to die are (1) psychologically different. We feel different about actively killing Aunt Mary than we do about allowing her to die by withdrawing or withholding treatments. (2) They differ also by intention. This refers to the whole purpose for doing something. Actively killing Aunt Mary is aiming at her death, whereas allowing her to die by withdrawing treatment is accepting our limitations to reverse the dying process and so lets the disease process run its course. (3) They differ in their long-range consequences. One possibility is that active killing for mercy may lead to active killing for other reasons. (4) The cause of death is different. Dr. Smith's causing Aunt Mary's death by giving a lethal injection is different from her dying by the progression of disease. (5) Killing conflicts with the role of the physician who professes to be a healer and preserver of life.

Veatch believes that while no one of these reasons alone can bear the weight of the distinction, all of them taken together do make a more convincing case that killing is morally different from allowing to die. Veatch admits that some of these arguments are more persuasive than others. In the end, the case for holding to a moral difference between killing and allowing to die rests upon all of these arguments taken together, not on any one alone.[3] However, Veatch does not believe that any of these arguments leads to the conclusion that killing is always wrong on balance. Even though killing is presumptively wrong, in rare cases it may be justified as an expression of justice to improve the situation of the least well-off, as in the case of the dying person in intractable pain.[4]

James Childress also believes the distinction between killing and allowing to die is worth retaining, but he argues that some acts of killing may be an expression of love, mercy, kindness, and care, as would be the case of killing to relieve pain which cannot be controlled and when the one in pain expresses a wish to be relieved of such misery.[5]

A Moral Difference

This brief survey of positions shows that some believe the distinction is simply a descriptive one, or a moral one that dissolves at a certain point in the process of dying. The Catholic tradition, however, holds firm to the distinction between killing and allowing to die all the way through the dying process. Its position is grounded in the principle of the sanctity of life. The Vatican *Declaration on Euthanasia* appeals to sanctity of life to frame its opposition to euthanasia: "Most people regard life as something sacred and hold that no one may dispose of it at will, but believers see in life something greater, namely a gift of God's love, which they are called upon to preserve and make fruitful"(I).

The church holds to this principle on religious and non-religious grounds. On religious grounds the principle of the sanctity of life means that the sacredness, sanctity, value, or dignity of human life is conferred by God. Each person is of incalculable worth and has dignity and value because we are made in the image of God, redeemed by Christ, and called to share fully in the life of the triune God. The dignity of human life entitles each person to the same basic right to life regardless of age or condition. The value and dignity of human life are guaranteed because they come solely from God creating us and sustaining us by love. Personal achievements, good moral character, economic status, social prestige, ethnic origins, legal fiat, or usefulness to others do not confer dignity. God does.

Although the theological foundation for the sanctity of life requires that all should affirm God as the source of this sanctity, the Catholic Church recognizes that the sacredness or sanctity of life may not be accepted by those who do not share its religious convictions. To promote the sanctity of life on nonreligious grounds, the Catholic moral tradition has appealed to the universal experience of the value of life inherent in all. Philosopher Edward Shils has argued along these lines to show that the sacredness or sanctity of life need not come from outside life but is grounded within the experience of life itself, "in the primordial experience of being alive, in the fear of extinction, in the spontaneous revulsion to contrived interventions and unnatural destruction of human life, and in the sense of awe one feels before one's vitality and that of the species."[6]

"Sanctity of life" affirms that physical life is a basic good because it is the fundamental condition which makes it possible to achieve all other values, and it sets the limits within which we must work to promote human well-being.

Two obligations are enshrined by "sanctity of life." The first is the positive obligation to nurture and support life. In the Vatican declaration this is expressed as the duty to lead a fruitful life. The second is the negative obligation not to harm or destroy life. In the declaration this is expressed by the prohibition against directly taking innocent life, which includes the prohibitions against euthanasia and suicide.

In short, "sanctity of life" creates a presumption in favor of sustaining life and so places the burden of proof on those who would take life or fail to forestall death. It also directs us to foster life-affirming attitudes and to scrutinize any discussion to terminate life or forgo life-sustaining treatment.

Intimately associated with the concept of sanctity of life are two other religious principles which support the obligations entailed in the sanctity of life principle. These are the principle of divine sovereignty and the principle expressed in the divine law, "You shall not kill."

The declaration affirms that intentionally causing death is a rejection of God's sovereignty over life. The principle of sovereignty acknowledges that we are the created and not the Creator. Human life is God's creation and our task, God's gift to us and our responsibility to cherish as a sacred trust. What makes killing forbidden is that it violates the right of divine ownership. For this reason, the Catholic tradition has regarded taking innocent human life as "intrinsically evil" by defect of right. No one can claim total mastery over one's own or another's life. As we saw above in responding to the argument from autonomy, sovereignty claims that human responsibility for life is one of stewardship, not ownership. Absolute dominion is an exclusively divine prerogative.

Closely related to the principles of sanctity and sovereignty is the divine law prohibiting killing as found in the fifth commandment. Scripture scholars tell us that the original significance of the precept against killing is hard to translate into English because we have no word that expresses the meaning of the Hebrew term now translated as "kill."[7] The commandment does not forbid killing in general, since the Israelite's larger religious-social code permitted killing of their enemies, killing for vengeance, or killing as punishment for a capital crime. The commandment seems to prohibit killing a fellow Israelite without the approval and deliberation of the entire community. This would certainly include murder and even accidental homicide. Although this precept clearly protects human life, it does not do so at the expense of the community's need to protect itself nor of God's claims over life.

The significance of appealing to this commandment in making a case against euthanasia, then, does not lie in the fact that it prohibits killing, since it does not prohibit killing in general. Rather, it protects the bonds of being a covenantal community by prohibiting the arbitrary taking of life by an individual, private decision, without community sanction.

Perhaps the greater significance of an appeal to divine law in making a case against euthanasia is seen when we read the fifth commandment in conjunction with the fourth, "Honor your father and mother." We miss the significance of this commandment if we understand it as requiring children to obey their parents. The original commandment was addressed to an adult community that was easily tempted, as a nomadic people, to leave behind or neglect anyone who was aged, feeble, senile, or useless in favor of clan members with greater mobility and vitality. This commandment indicates that human honor and worth are innate to our relation to God and to others who are interdependent partners with us in a covenantal community. Within covenantal bonds, honor and worth are not dependent on social usefulness.

Thus the divine law against killing, when taken in conjunction with the commandment to honor father and mother, provides a fuller expression of the value of human life being affirmed and protected within a covenantal commitment. Together, the commandments emphasize that the human family belongs to a covenantal community wherein the full capacity for being human flourishes by maintaining bonds of trust. Any support for euthanasia in such a community would need to account for the commitment we have to one another to protect and to promote each other within trustworthy relationships. To accept responsibility for one's own life and that of others is an expression of this covenantal commitment. Caring for each other's life is a sign, under God, of the trust everyone must have toward one another if life is to flourish.

Two other dimensions of the prohibition against killing integral to the Catholic opposition to euthanasia are implied in the declaration's definition of euthanasia: "an action or an omission which of itself or by intention causes death, in order that all suffering may in this way be eliminated." "Methods" and "intention" identify the two key dimensions of this Catholic position.

"Methods" refers to "an action or an omission" causing death. Actions that cause death are fairly easy to recognize. In instances of euthanasia or physician-assisted suicide, these actions are usually lethal doses of narcotic drugs by injection or pills. Omissions that cause death are sometimes harder to recognize because they can be confused with the acceptable withholding of treatment. An unacceptable omission that is morally equivalent to killing is the failure to provide lifesaving treatment that would significantly reverse a debilitating condition, bring reasonable relief with tolerable burden, and prevent someone's death. Such was the case with Baby Doe who had Down's syndrome and an esophageal fistula which could have been repaired easily to make feeding possible. But it wasn't, and the baby was allowed to die. This was a case of euthanasia by omission. An acceptable omission, however, is omitting a medical intervention which is futile and/or too burdensome for the patient, thus allowing the patient to die from natural causes such as withdrawing a respirator from a comatose person with end-stage brain cancer. The Catholic position is that allowing a person to die by omitting futile or disproportionately burdensome treatment is morally different from killing and is not euthanasia.

The second term of reference on which the definition of euthanasia turns is "intention." The declaration's use of "intention" follows standard Catholic moral teaching and interpretation of "You shall not kill." What is forbidden is to "intend the death of an innocent person" or "to choose death as your end or means to your end."

In the Catholic moral tradition, "intention" designates the whole purpose for doing something. Intention does not mean motive, which refers to the emotional influences on us. Intention answers the question, "What are we really doing here?" It includes a reasoned decision about a goal and the means to achieve it. So, if I intend to kill you, then I have decided that my goal is your death, and I have decided how to bring your death about. The declaration applies this understanding in addressing a question like this: Can Dr. Smith administer a pain-relieving drug to Aunt Mary knowing that the drug may cause or hasten her death, even though death is not the outcome he seeks? The Vatican declaration addressed such a scenario and quoted from a 1957 address of Pius XII:

> In answer to a group of doctors who had put the question: "Is the suppression of pain and consciousness by the use of narcotics permitted by religion and morality to the doctor and the patient (even at the approach of death and if one foresees that the use of narcotics will shorten life)?"

The Pope said, "If no other means exist, and if, in the given circumstances, this does not prevent the carrying out of other religious and moral duties: Yes." (III)

Justification for this position is based on the application of the principle of double effect. According to this principle, Dr. Smith's intention is to protect the good of Aunt Mary's life by bringing her relief from pain. The foreseeable yet unwanted side effect is her death. The prohibition against killing applies to "intentional" killing—a deliberately sought and caused death. The prohibition, therefore, does not apply to the unwanted side effect of death which comes about as a result of relieving pain. Catholic teaching maintains, and the principle of double effect affirms, that if the act or omission's ultimate goal is to produce death or is the means to our goal (killing to relieve suffering), then the act or omission is morally wrong. Death may be morally tolerated when it is the inevitable side effect resulting from using medication to relieve pain.[8]

The distinction between killing and allowing to die is supported by Daniel Callahan's argument against euthanasia in a climate which finds it an attractive way to control unwanted medical costs, especially for the dying and the critically ill.[9] He correctly shows that the euthanasia and rationing debates mutually influence one another. The effect of rationing decisions will be that some patients will be allowed to die whose lives might otherwise be prolonged. Without upholding the distinction we cannot have a sensible allocation debate.

At the heart of Callahan's approach is the difference between human responsibility for death and the physical causality of death. The distinction separates deaths caused by impersonal forces for which no one can be held responsible, and deaths caused by human action for which someone can be held morally culpable. To deny the distinction is to assume that all of nature falls under human control. To defend the distinction, Callahan appeals to three different perspectives on nature and human action: metaphysical, moral, and medical.

The *metaphysical perspective* is based on a real difference between us and the external world, which has its own causal dynamism. As a result, we cannot have unlimited control over everything. Modern medicine, for example, can intervene to forestall death for a time, but not forever. The limitations of the body are ultimately beyond final human control. To deny the distinction between killing and allowing to die concedes more power to human intervention than we actually have.

The *moral perspective* draws a line between physical causality and human responsibility. The line separates deaths caused by impersonal forces (the disease causes death) for which no one can be held responsible, and deaths caused by human action (a lethal injection causes death) for which someone can be held morally culpable. However, in some instances the lines cross when we are just as culpable in killing someone as we are in allowing someone to die whom we have an obligation to save. The death of Baby Doe is a case in point. It illustrates that the mere fact that death results from an action or an omission is not sufficient to determine whether it is morally acceptable. But the fact that the lines can cross in some instances does not show that killing and allowing to die are always one and the same. For example, the distinction has moral bite in those instances where, with good moral reason, life-prolonging measures are removed from Dad when his failing heart and kidneys can no longer carry out ordinary biological functions on their own. In these instances the irreversible incapacitating disease is the cause of death.

The medical perspective underscores the social purpose of the distinction. It protects the role of physicians as the ones who use their knowledge of the body and diseases to cure or comfort patients rather than to kill them. Physicians' power over life should be limited to curing and comforting. To extend their power to killing would violate what it means to be a physician.

CONCLUSION

These various perspectives on the distinction between killing and allowing to die are momentous for the euthanasia debate. If there is no moral distinction between killing and allowing to die, then every decision to withhold or withdraw futile or overly burdensome treatment can be construed as direct killing. If that were so, then we have greased the slide toward a general policy of euthanasia. However, those who admit that the distinction does not hold under all circumstances (such as in the manner of Paul Ramsey), and so concede a qualified acceptance of an "exceptional-case" euthanasia under certain conditions, do not have to conclude that justifying one act of euthanasia leads to justifying a social policy for the general practice of euthanasia. Tom Beauchamp and James Childress, along with the President's Commission for the Study of Ethical Problems in Medicine and Biomedical and Behavioral Research (1978–1983), have argued that it may be necessary to have a policy restricting the taking of life in extreme circumstances, even when the action does not appear to be wrong, in order to avoid the undesirable consequences of the unjustified taking of life in less extreme circumstances.[10]

4. BENEFICENCE

Closely following the argument from autonomy and the calling into question the prohibition against killing and the moral difference between killing and allowing to die, especially in the case of truly tormented dying patients, supporters of euthanasia also argue from the desire to relieve the patient of suffering a life deemed no longer worth living. This brings us within the scope of beneficence which includes the duty to help others in need and to avoid harm, but always within the limits of the commitment of the medical profession to care for the sick.

Three dimensions of the scope of beneficence have played a prominent role in the euthanasia debate: the "character" of medicine as a profession; the "suffering" that is to be relieved; and the "mercy" that is to be shown the suffering/dying.

THE CHARACTER OF MEDICINE

The argument for euthanasia from beneficence brings us to the moral center of medicine. At stake is the social conception of the role of the physician and the very aim of medicine. That we cannot reach a moral consensus on euthanasia reflects the disagreement on these matters. We do not have unanimity today on the expectations attached to the physician's role and on the boundaries of the commitment of medicine. The euthanasia debate raises the question of whether killing patients is the physician's business and so fits within the aim of medicine.

At the present time, only three groups of people are sanctioned by society to kill—the military, the police, and public executioners of capital punishment. If euthanasia were legalized, we would add physicians to this list. But would doing that be compatible with the goals of the medical profession? That society has not permitted physicians to serve as public executioners reflects the common sense wisdom and Hippocratic tradition that "doctors must not kill." Yet both this wisdom and tradition are being called into question in the name of being merciful to those suffering at the end of life.

Dr. Timothy Quill has become a prominent spokesman challenging this wisdom and tradition since his article justifying assisting his patient Diane in her decision to commit suicide appeared in the nation's most prestigious medical journal, *The New England Journal of Medicine*. Dr. Quill's argument was that "the preoccupation with her fear of a lingering death would interfere with Diane's getting the most out of the time she had left until she found a safe way to ensure her death."[1] His argument makes clear that he used his medical skills to treat not only her medical needs, but also to satisfy her value of life and her desire to live in a particular way. His justification takes him beyond the physician's traditional role of using specialized knowledge and skill to treat medical needs and reaches into the realm of judging what kind of life is worth living.

Opponents to physicians becoming killers argue on the basis of the traditional aim of medicine and the responsibilities proper to the physician's social role. Albert Jonsen, for example, has argued on the basis of the social expectations and responsibilities attached to the physician's role that "being a physician" and "killing a patient" have nothing to do with each other. According to him, the appropriate professional role of the physician "is to use scientific knowledge and clinical experience in making decisions and advising patients about the prevention, diagnosis, and treatment of disease and the maintenance of health."[2] The killing of a patient by lethal injection is not a proper medical skill.

Similarly, Leon Kass argues that the role of the physician is defined by the goal of medicine—to benefit the wholeness of one who is sick. For him the physician-euthanizer is self-contradictory. Intentionally killing the patient does not fit within the physician's aim to promote healing and wholeness. For a physician to be acting to benefit the patient presupposes that the patient will survive in order to be the beneficiary of the physician's activity of healing. Kass puts it this way:

> Can one benefit the patient as a whole by making him dead? There is, of course, a logical difficulty: how can any good exist for a being that is not? But the error is more than logical: to intend and to act for someone's good requires his continued existence to receive the benefit.[3]

Daniel Callahan also argues that euthanasia is incompatible with the goal of medicine and the competence of the physician:

> Doctors ought to relieve those forms of suffering that medically accompany serious illness and the threat of death. They should relieve pain, do what they can to allay anxiety and uncertainty, and be a comforting presence.[4]

According to Callahan, physicians who euthanize or assist in suicide have moved beyond medicine's proper realm of promoting and preserving health and into the metaphysical realm of determining the value of life and what kind of lives are worth living. This broader realm of what makes for general human happiness is a matter of religion or philosophy. It does not belong to medicine's competence. Callahan holds to the conviction that, while it is the proper role of medicine to relieve the suffering caused by physical pain or psychological stressors that may accompany sickness, it does not belong to medicine to judge the kind of life worth living when a person suffers from despair in the human condition.[5]

Arguments such as those developed by Jonsen, Kass, and Callahan support the moral character of medicine as a commitment to healing which is incompatible with doctors killing patients. By wanting to license physicians to kill, advocates of euthanasia are calling into question the social expectations of the physician and the moral character of medical practice. The traditional aim for medicine to prevent disease and to restore or maintain health fits well within the Catholic tradition's limits of the scope of the prohibition against killing outlined in the last chapter. Thus, the Catholic perspective views the moral character of the medical profession to be incompatible with euthanasia and physician-assisted suicide.

SUFFERING

Another dimension to the argument from beneficence is the appeal to the obligation to relieve suffering. Next to the right to choose how and when we die, a fundamental claim of the euthanasia movement is the obligation we have to one another to relieve suffering, especially unnecessary and meaningless suffering. The Vatican declaration links euthanasia with the experience of suffering by defining euthanasia as causing death "in order that all suffering may in this way be eliminated" (II).

The argument from suffering reaches beyond medicine's physical boundaries of promoting and preserving health or wholeness and into the boundless metaphysical realm of general human happiness or a "meaningful" life. People ask to be released from life through euthanasia or medically assisted suicide because they judge that the life they now have with the suffering they must now endure has no value, has lost meaning. Such was the case with Dr. Quill's patient, Diane. To enlist a physician in achieving release from a meaningless life of suffering as she did presumes the physician is competent to judge what kinds of life are worth living.

Perhaps this would be true if suffering had only medical causes. As Eric Cassell's analysis of suffering shows, while physical pain may be the major physical cause of suffering, the root problem of suffering and mortality is more than physical.[6] The degree and intensity to which people suffer, and whether they find life empty or meaningless, turns less on their physical condition and more on their outlook on life. Suffering is more a personal matter in the sense that it is a function of a person's attitude and framework of meaning than it is an unpleasant experience. While we should not be glorifying suffering or seeking it as an end, we can make it less overwhelming by framing it in the context of a life that has value and is supported by strong bonds of love. This helps explain how Aunt Vera and Uncle Frank, two people with the same heart disease, the same physician, and the same hospital had such different experiences of suffering. Uncle Frank found it unbearable. Aunt Vera did not. Her outlook on life was informed by religious convictions which enabled her to situate the physical condition within a hopeful framework of meaning.

Questions in the minds and hearts, and often on the lips, of those suffering from pain, such as, "How can I bear this pain?" "Why am I suffering?" "Why must I die?" can be asked as medical questions with physical answers. But they can also be asked as religious questions about the meaning of life. Medicine can rightly address the physical causes of pain, suffering, and death, and it ought to do so. But beyond that physicians have no special competence to address the suffering which arises from despairing in the human condition. Nor do they have any special competence to address the questions of meaning which facing the limits of being human raises.

The meaning of pain, suffering, and death is tied to the meaning of life itself. This is fundamentally a religious question. What makes finding meaning in pain, suffering, and death hard today is that our scientific interventions to resist them have put aside any religious meaning that might give us the courage to face them. As religious believers, however, we can retrieve from our tradition a vision of faith as a context of meaning for facing pain, suffering, and death with humility, courage, and hope. The Catholic tradition teaches that, while we should take reasonable steps to stay healthy and to prevent death, when this is not possible the convictions of faith enable us to find meaning in suffering and thereby transform it. The Rite for the Pastoral Care of the Sick states:

> Christians feel and experience pain as do all other people; yet their faith helps them to grasp more deeply the mystery of suffering and to bear their pain with greater courage. From Christ's words they know that sickness has meaning and value for their own salvation and for the salvation of the world. (Intro, no. 1)

This perspective shows that the acceptance of suffering is an experience of faith, an experience of trusting in the mysteriousness of God. With this awareness of the links between faith and suffering, the church focuses the season of Lent, especially Good Friday, around the theme of suffering so that we might annually enter into its mystery through ritual and prayer.

When we cannot turn to religious perspectives on suffering to address these questions, we can easily reduce the cause of suffering or the questions of meaning to purely physical ones. On the physical plane, a physician's lethal injection becomes the answer to the meaning of life. From the religious perspective, this only makes euthanasia the wrong answer and given by the wrong people. Religious faith helps us to grasp the mystery of suffering as a moment for closer bonding with God in Christ. To approach suffering as an opportunity to identify with the suffering of Christ can be the way of finding meaning in the experience of distress from a deteriorating physical condition.

The Catholic tradition teaches that suffering, while not a value in itself but an experience of evil, can be transformed.[7] The foundation for finding meaning in suffering lies in the dignity of the human person as one fashioned in the divine image (Gen 1:26). As bearers of God's image, our dignity is never lost, even when we are diminished by disease and pain. The mystery of the incarnation, especially God's loving embrace of humanity through Jesus on the cross, opens the way to the transformation of suffering. The life-death-resurrection of Jesus assures us that God has entered every aspect of human existence, even suffering and death. The passion of Christ reminds us that every fear and misery, even the suffering during the last moments of life, have a direct and redemptive relationship with Jesus and so is taken up into God's love.

The Vatican declaration speaks of suffering during the last moments of life as having a special place in God's plan: "It is in fact a sharing in Christ's passion and a union with the redeeming sacrifice which he offered in obedience to the father's will" (III). Pope John Paul II affirmed as much in his letter, *The Christian Meaning of Human Suffering*:

One can say that with the passion of Christ all human suffering has found itself in a new situation...In the cross of
Christ not only is the Redemption accomplished through
suffering, but also human suffering itself has been
redeemed. (no. 19)[8]

The story of the life-death-resurrection of Jesus tells us
that the tragedy of suffering and dying is transformed.
Suffering and death cannot, and will not, be stronger than
God's love. The story of Jesus tells us, as well, that suffering
and death do not have the last word. Suffering reminds us
that God's reign is not yet final, and the risen One invites us
to participate in resurrected life. Our belief that Christ has
been raised from the dead is also our hope that suffering and
death can be and will be transformed into the fullness of life.
God's love, revealed in the resurrection of Jesus, gives us the
courage to enter into suffering and death knowing that life
ultimately triumphs. If, through suffering, the sufferer is
brought nearer to God in Christ, then that person may bear
it courageously because of the comfort of the spiritual experience it offers. The bonding with Christ is the means for
managing the suffering well.

MERCY

The scope of beneficence is ultimately about mercy, that
is, about how we fulfill the demands of covenantal fidelity
that we owe one another. What kind of mercy toward the
dying fits the commitment first to be faithful and then to be
healing whenever possible? While it may be inappropriate
to speak of killing as healing, may it yet be compatible with
mercy toward those who are dying in pain and find life
empty, oppressive, and meaningless? Those who argue in
support of euthanasia think so.

But our biblical witness of mercy and compassion points us in a different direction. In the Bible, mercy and compassion represent the way that God maintains covenantal fidelity with the chosen people. God's mercy is the fulfillment of the covenantal commitment to be with and for the chosen people in all circumstances. Mercy and compassion are the ways that God, who had covenanted with Israel, continues to love her, provides for her, and protects her from harm. Mercy is always available to the people of the covenant because of God's faithfulness to them. In the life of Jesus, mercy and compassion led him to do works which restored the broken to wholeness. Out of mercy and compassion, he healed the blind, taught the ignorant, raised the dead, and fed the hungry.[9]

The biblical witness to mercy shows us that deep personal relationships lie at the heart of divine and human mercy. Those who are especially dependent on the community, such as children, the aged, and the poor, have a special claim on mercy because without communal support, they are helpless. Stanley Hauerwas, a theologian noted for his emphasis on the importance of being a virtuous community, argues against euthanasia on the basis of our being partners in a covenantal community.[10] Those practicing medicine embody the virtue of fidelity in their commitment to be partners in a caring community and to be present and not to abandon those they cannot cure.

To resort to euthanasia is to fail to embody the trust that sustains life and the commitment to be companions to one another, especially those who are helpless or those who are unable to contribute to the community. The refusal to participate in euthanasia is a reminder and an encouragement to remain committed to one another as partners who sustain each other through trust, mercy, and care. An important expression of a merciful community is to provide the structures and to develop the skills which will enable us to be present to those who suffer. We must let them know that they remain partners with us in this interdependent covenantal community of trust and care.

We believe that the human family is a community constituted by the story of God's promise to love manifested in the calling of Israel and in the life of Jesus. The sense of our being made in the image of God finds its fullest expression in our capacity to enter into covenant with God and with one another. As members of a covenantal community bound together in love, God calls each person to be responsible to and for one another. Enduring loyalty, trust, and mercy are the virtues which express this responsibility in a community of care, especially in those instances when medicine has reached its limits to cure.

The demand for euthanasia will increase if structures of support and skills of care do not keep pace with the demand. By facing our limits to heal, we as a community of care can do much to benefit the lives of the dying without resorting to euthanasia. We must address more effectively the "need" for euthanasia, such as by providing adequate relief of pain, by withholding or withdrawing treatments that only prolong dying, by keeping company with those who are lonely, and by being a resource of meaning and hope for those tempted to despair.

The demand for euthanasia is a reminder that we are failing as a community both to embody the trust and mercy that sustains life and to live out the commitment to be companions to one another, especially those who are most dependent on us because of their own helplessness. If we as a community want to stand squarely against euthanasia, then we have a covenantal responsibility to provide the support structures and the skills needed to help one another to live when life is hard.

Although we believe that the death and resurrection of Jesus Christ has deprived death of its power as an absolute evil, we do not believe that causing death to end suffering is compatible with our covenantal commitment to one another to be faithful, trusting, and merciful. Death signifies that humans are ultimately powerless before God. Each person dies in utter dependence on God. Euthanasia signals the refusal to accept this powerlessness and dependence. Euthanasia is a death-oriented solution to the problems of how to care for the dying. The challenge and task for those who care for the suffering/dying is to show them that they are not abandoned by the human community or by God.

CONCLUSION

Character, suffering, and mercy are three aspects of the scope of beneficence which are at issue in the euthanasia debate. The Catholic religious and moral tradition supports the traditional moral center of medicine which finds killing incompatible with the commitment to heal. Faith informed by the biblical stories of covenant and the life-death-resurrection of Jesus provides a special context of meaning within which to understand suffering and mercy. In the eyes of faith, suffering need not diminish the dignity of the human person. The Christian faith invites those who suffer to grasp its deeper mystery. Faith offers a chance to transform the uselessness of suffering by identifying with the suffering of Christ and thereby coming to a closer bonding with God in Christ. Mercy fulfills the demands of covenantal fidelity by not killing but by companioning with compassion those who suffer. Mercy embodies the trust and care that supports the suffering/dying from not abandoning hope when life is hard.

5. A PASTORAL RESPONSE

The preceding chapters have surveyed the leading arguments for and against euthanasia and assisted suicide. They emphasized the principles to which we can appeal in helping us to decide what we are going to do about personal requests for euthanasia or public appeals to legalize euthanasia. Now it is time to "walk the talk," as it were, if our principles and arguments are ever going to be convincing.

This last chapter aims to bring the euthanasia debate closer to home by focusing on what a pastoral response to the euthanasia movement might look like. To do this we will have to move from in-principled arguments to the depths of moral character and spirituality. How we live with mortality is, at root, a profoundly religious issue. It is a matter of our outlook on life and habits of being, all rolled into one.

This pastoral response is based on the conviction that, in moral matters, witness is more compelling than arguments. Principles may teach, but shining examples make principles come alive and influence public opinion more strongly. Why? Because we learn morality primarily through real life people and their stories which have a fascinating appeal to the moral imagination. The reason for this is simple. We are not angels. Angels might begin with the abstract, "No direct killing of the innocent." But we begin with Uncle Charlie. We learn through experience and by example. No wonder, then, that what often makes our moral positions unconvincing is not the logic of our principles but our example, which ultimately gives living meaning to our convictions. The true significance of our Catholic opposition to euthanasia ultimately rests on the kind of witness that runs ahead of and behind the convictions which we say make euthanasia untenable. In order to be a credible player in the debate, then, we have to bear convincing witness, personally and corporately, to the way we care for the sick, the elderly, the dying, and the unsuccessful. What kind of persons and community should we be in order to encourage people to view death as an inevitable outcome that no one needs to hasten through lethal intervention?

From Principles to Virtue

Appealing to principles in order to decide what to do in the face of a moral bind is only one part of the field of ethics. By itself, the appeal does not offer enough insight into what kind of person we must be in order to face our death without thinking about euthanasia, or what the community as a whole must be like in order to deal with dying and death in ways that would not lead us to hasten death through lethal intervention.

T. S. Eliot once pointed to this other level in ethics that will give us insight into a pastoral response to the euthanasia movement. After lecturing on a serious issue in American life, he was asked, "Mr. Eliot, what are we going to do about the problem you have discussed?" He replied, in effect, "You have asked the wrong question. You must understand that we face two types of problems in life. One kind of problem provokes the question, 'What are we going to do about it?' The other kind poses a subtler question, 'How do we behave towards it?'"[1] The first type of problem demands a response of the sort developed in the earlier chapters on principles. The second type poses a deeper challenge which no in-principled argument or political strategy can reach. The challenge is not to find something to do, but to find someone to be.

The demands of facing sickness, debilitation, fading powers, and death require more than skilled techniques of medicine. They also require a certain kind of character. When my dad was dying, I saw that there was nothing anyone in our family could do, skilled though we may have been in medicine, education, or religion. The real issue we had to face was whether we could rise to the occasion to face this unwanted circumstance. Whether we could or not depended a great deal on our outlook on life, or what some would call the "character" of our family. A crisis, such as a critical, life-threatening illness, certainly confronts us with things to do. But far more profoundly, such a crisis forces us to be in a certain way.

Who we will be in the face of such a crisis will reflect who we have become up to that point. Who we will be is a matter of what we have come to believe about life, the values we uphold, the attitudes we take, and the kind of persons our patterns of thought and behavior have helped us to become. If we have not already developed habits of the heart for facing unwanted yet encroaching deprivations that occur in life, then we will not have them to strengthen us in the face of death.

The euthanasia movement is as much a challenge to the depth of moral character as it is a challenge to the meaning of our moral principles. But matters of character and "outlook on life," or one's spirituality, are kept out of the public debates. Yet, cutting across the debates over ways to change the law, to refine moral reasoning, or to revise medical practice in the face of dying are fundamental issues that define our outlook on life and moral character. What constitutes a meaningful life; how should I want to live in order to die well; what kind of person do I want to be in the face of suffering; how much suffering must I be willing to bear and for what reason; what kind of person should I be in order to make room for the weak and unsuccessful; do I want to be the kind of person who insists on controlling everything; how should I think about my relationship with others; what do I owe others in my dying?

Many of our problems with reaching an agreement on the public policy and the morality of euthanasia stem from our positions on these sorts of questions. So, when we begin to consider how we might effectively respond to the euthanasia movement, we need to include not only the soundness of our principles but also the spiritual depths and strength of our character.

In order to fashion a pastoral response to the euthanasia movement, this chapter begins by sketching with a broad brush the conditions that can be brought on by sickness, serious debilitation, or the weakness of old age that could make one feel hopeless and want to bring about death quickly and effectively through euthanasia or assisted suicide. Against the background of these conditions of hopelessness, can we then sketch an outlook on life formed by some virtues of personal and corporate character that we need to foster so that euthanasia wouldn't even come to mind.

CONDITIONS OF HOPELESSNESS

Often the physical, emotional, social, and spiritual constraints that accompany sickness, debilitation, or weakness from old age do not open to any attractive possibilities for living. They create conditions of hopelessness that make euthanasia or assisted suicide seem like the right thing to do. These conditions of hopelessness can be experienced in a variety of ways. But three large categories seem to cover the territory generally: 1) the loss of control; 2) the loss of meaning in suffering; 3) the loss of human connection.

The Loss of Control

A sense of hopelessness can easily overcome us when we have no say in determining the course of our lives or in shaping the events in which we participate. Losing control easily follows upon the physical and emotional constraints that accompany illness or old age. When we become preoccupied with trying to achieve physical comfort or emotional balance, we can easily lose our sense of being able to take charge of our lives. Physically we lie open to being an object of invasion and manipulation. Emotionally we are discouraged when we are not able to satisfy any of our goals. We ask in desperation, "If I can't see how I am ever going to better the condition I am now in, why live? If I am more a victim of others' invasive and manipulative procedures rather than an agent seeking my own desires, why survive?"

The Loss of Meaning in Suffering

Another sense of hopelessness can overcome us when we no longer feel we are of value or have any meaningful goals to achieve. If our days are filled with a boring routine, and we play no significant part in shaping the day, then our strength to live weakens. If our suffering does not fit into any larger scheme of meaning, and if it serves no purpose for us or anyone else, then it feels like living itself has lost its purpose. It seems pointless to go on, and no one can go on without purpose. Religious faith is often a significant resource for coping with suffering, since it is one of the major influences shaping the attitudes we bring to the experience. Anyone who feels disconnected with the transcendent source of meaning experiences what the psalmist and, later, Jesus put more bluntly, "My God, my God, why have you forsaken me?" Suffering almost inevitably calls us to reappraise our faith. But can a new and stronger faith be built?

The Loss of Human Connection

When we are "fully alive," does our reason for living lie in some conceptual certainty of what life is about? Or, does it not lie rather in being included in a network of supportive relationships, in being touched by another, in being valued as a person? Hopelessness can readily overcome us when we are cut off from those relationships which help us to appreciate life as a gift sustained by the love of another. The isolation may be self-inflicted, such as when our pride denies a need for others in the name of being self-sufficient. Or, it may come from the inattention of family, friends, and care givers who are preoccupied by their own interests and obligations. In either case, when we no longer experience a mutual interdependence with work companions, social groups, and family which once sustained a meaningful life, and when living becomes only a task carried out as a duty, why try to live any longer?

These conditions of hopelessness—a loss of control, a loss of meaning in suffering, and a loss of human contact—make euthanasia an attractive way out. A pastoral response to the euthanasia movement must be able to address these conditions personally and corporately. It is to personal and corporate virtues that we turn now to sketch a pastoral response to the euthanasia movement.

PERSONAL VIRTUES

The virtuous approach to dying believes that we will die the way we have lived. Daniel Callahan has it exactly right when he asserts that we cannot guarantee how we will react to the prospects of suffering and dying, but we can begin to shape the self we will bring to that experience. He says, "How we die will be an expression of how we have wanted to live, and the meaning we have found in our dying will be at one with the meaning we have found in our living."[2] Therefore, even now when death seems like "a distant thunder on a summer's day," as W. H. Auden once put it, I can still prepare to face death by working to become the kind of person I want to bring to it. I need not be a mere victim of what dying has in store for me. Rather, I can actively engage my dying by developing those habits of the heart which will make a difference in the way I adapt to unwanted circumstances and endure what I cannot change. If we do not develop these habits for living throughout our life, then we will not have them to strengthen us in the face of death. So what kind of person do we want to bring to our sickness, suffering, and decline in order to make euthanasia unthinkable?

Humility

Humility does not come easily to Americans. We bridle at limits, especially moral limits. The sketch of autonomy in Chapter 2 showed that the core ideal of the self which the individualism of our culture upholds is a self whose dignity and worth is pinned on independence and freedom to control outcomes. The spiritual question this raises is, "To what extent do I want to live out the vision that sees only an independent life of absolute control as a life worth living?"

Certainly, no one wants to deny that we need some degree of control if we are to respect personal dignity. In modern medicine, we must be able to make choices. Otherwise, we could easily be used and abused by medical bureaucracy and the technological domination of medicine. The freedom we prize and protect in culture and in medicine is more the freedom to control outcomes than it is the freedom to choose an attitude. Viktor Frankl called the capacity to remain our own person in the face of what is given the "last of the human freedoms—to choose one's attitude in any given set of circumstances, to choose one's own way."[3] This is the freedom of the virtue of humility.

Our ascetical tradition offers a view of life which is quite different from that supported by modern individualism. It is carried by the virtue of humility, the virtue that will check our passion for control by enabling us to take a lighter grasp on life. When talking about humility we must be careful not to confuse it with that false humility which is a kind of spiritual masochism—self-defacement, submissive servility, or infantile docility.

To understand humility properly as a virtue, it helps to remember that humility, human, and earth have the same word root—*humus*. God took the dust of the earth, breathed into it, and brought forth the "earth creature" (Gen 2:7). We have been destined for humility ever since: "Remember, you are dust and unto dust you shall return." Humility, simply put, is being down to earth about ourselves. It does not try to run ahead of our graces and make of ourselves more than we are. It graciously accepts ourselves as creatures and God as Creator. It is able to live with limits, to stand back when it is time, and to trust in the gracious work of God. Obvious as that seems, it often takes illness or death to impress the idea on our minds. We are mortal, "vessels of clay" (2 Cor 4:7), fragile, and ultimately powerless. Only God is without limit.

Humility enables us to retain a sense of worth and dignity without having absolute control. It emphasizes our capacity to live with limits, to choose a stance towards the hand we have been handed, and to stand back and to let go of what cannot be ours. The person who learns how to live within the limits that come with being creature, and the person who can let go of what does not belong to us is the person who will be able to face with openness and flexibility the limits of being social and being mortal.

As social persons, we must accept our mutual interdependence. Others have claims on us. Humility does not regard becoming dependent an indignity. Accepting dependence could be a growing process, not a wilting one. Jesus showed in his suffering the dignity of dependence. In Gethsemane, we hear him plead with his disciples, "The sorrow in my heart is so great that it almost crushes me. Stay here and keep watch with me" (Matt 26:38). This dependence on others is a sign of a more radical dependence on God, for Jesus then threw himself on the ground and prayed, "My Father, if it is possible, take this cup of suffering from me! Yet not what I want, but what you want" (Matt 26:39). Jesus shows that dependence is a call to be open to God, to see more clearly the limits of control. Humility recognizes that leaning on the strength of others and being open to their care is a necessary grace. Humility lives with the tension between dependence and independence.

As mortal persons, we must face the fact that life is inevitably marked by illness, aging, decline, and death. The humble person knows that reality will ultimately go its own way and follow its own internal dynamism. To die with dignity, the humble do not need to be in charge of every detail. The humble only need to be in charge of the interior self so as to integrate into life the unexpected as well as the unwanted circumstances of life. Acquiring the virtue of humility as a desirable goal is one step towards making euthanasia something we wouldn't even imagine.

Courage

Courage is a companion of humility. If humility enables us to be realistic about our mortal limits, then courage enables us to "take heart" and face them. Courage acknowledges that our human condition has the capacity to hurt us. But courage refuses to allow this capacity to prevent us from taking a stance toward our condition despite our being hurt. When we "take heart" we draw upon our inward dignity which compensates for the lack of absolute control over nature, fate, and even death.

It is normal to be afraid of dying. We rightly fear death because we lose so much in it: we lose the people we love, the work we like to do, and all that gladdened our hearts. As Vatican II's *Constitution on the Church in the Modern World* pointed out, we do not want the total disappearance that death brings, yet we cannot ultimately control or avoid death from happening (no. 18). No wonder we feel angry when we get sick, have pain, suffer, and especially when we discover that we are dying. Anger, though, can give rise to attacking what threatens us with all the fierceness of heroic measures that modern medicine can offer. When those fail, euthanasia and assisted suicide can become attractive means of certain relief.

Courage combats anger by reflecting a contrasting way of dealing with what threatens so that we can face our own death. While courage supports the reasonable effort to prevent death, it also empowers us to live with limits and to cope with the darkness that envelops us when the possibility of being restored to health is out of the question. A Mercy sister who recently died of leukemia demonstrated such courage as she faced the reality of her death. Throughout her life, she was a woman of creativity, vision, and spirit. She put all that to use in the way she chose to live while dying. One of her passions in life was to develop a center of spirituality. She pursued that to the end. Even when she could no longer walk, she took to a motorized scooter to traverse the hallways to make real her dream. She was an inspiration to her whole community with the way she drew on her character and the inward dignity of her interior life to live and to love as long as she could. Such courage in the face of death comes only with encouragement from others to protect the human spirit against despair and defeat, not only at the time of dying but all through life. Encouraged by her community to pursue her dream, she had the courage to live well while dying.

In our Promethean society, which feeds on the myth that everything can be conquered, it takes courage to face up to this myth as an illusion. The reality is that we will experience pain, suffering, and death as the price of being human. But in our death-denying society, courage in the face of death does not come easily. If we avoid facing death, we never really learn how to live, nor how to die. M. Scott Peck found in his practice of psychotherapy that he had to push half his patients to face the reality of their death. Their reluctance to do so was part of their illness. He concludes, "We cannot live with courage and confidence until we can have a relationship with our own death. Indeed, we cannot live fully unless there is something we are willing to die for."[4]

Rollo May, in his book *The Courage to Create*,[5] describes the anatomy of courage for creative genius, but his attributes can be adapted to anyone who is facing the limits of mortality. *Physical* courage enables us to be in touch with our bodies rather than to want to master them with machines. *Moral* courage is the willingness to face the truth about our situation, to take the next step to change what we can, and then to accept what cannot be changed. *Social* courage is not afraid to share fears, fantasies, hopes, and doubts, to ask for help, or to bear another's burdens. *Creative* courage faces the darkness of pain and death with hope. It enables us to let go so that new forms of life may rise from the darkness. These dimensions of courage converge into one single dynamic in order to engage the whole person in a cure, if that is to be, or in accepting what cannot be cured but only endured.

Courage encourages us to integrate the fact of death into our view of life, but courage does not try to pretend that we can make everyone's death easy or that the loss that comes with death is not real. Courage enables us to face the reality of death with hope.

Hope

The knowledge that life is limited, that death is inevitable, fills many with a sense of meaninglessness. Like Qoheleth, we feel "All is vanity" (Eccl 1:2). Or we lament with Shakespeare's Macbeth, "Life's but a walking shadow. It is a tale told by an idiot, full of sound and fury, signifying nothing." Can that be? Does death wipe everything away?

Hope imagines what is possible even in the face of limitation and death. Hope is rooted in the biblical truth that all possibilities for life and its future stem from the fundamental graciousness of God's love which is constant and undefeatable. This is most clearly evident in Jesus being raised from the dead, our ultimate guarantee of hope. "If Christ has not been raised from death," St. Paul writes, "then we have nothing to preach and you have nothing to believe" (1 Cor 15:13). We proclaim our faith in the resurrection in our eucharistic acclamations, "Dying you destroyed our death, rising you restored our life. Lord Jesus come in glory"; and again, "Lord, by your cross and resurrection, you have set us free. You are the Savior of the world."

The resurrection of Jesus encourages us to hope that we will enjoy a new life beyond the grave. This hope in new life means that whatever we have now is not all that there is. Jesus' resurrection is the victory over suffering and death. We bank on its promise that all that we know now will be transformed by God into something new. To live with this resurrection-hope is to see that suffering and dying are not just pain and confusion, or merely the end. Hope sees them as an occasion for opening ourselves to God as the source and end of life. If we can nurture this hope, which assures us that there is more to life than what we experience now, we may be more ready to accept death when its time comes without the need to prolong it or to hasten it.

This vision of faith does not come spontaneously or easily. It often entails a struggle with periods of doubt and feelings of abandonment. This struggle is well illustrated by C.S. Lewis. At the beginning of Act Two of *Shadowlands*, Lewis is giving one of his public talks at the time he is trying to cope with the agony of his wife's dying in the hospital from advanced bone cancer. He says,

> I find it hard to believe that God loves her. If you love someone, you don't want them to suffer. You can't bear it. You want to take their suffering onto yourself. If even I feel like that, why doesn't God? Not just once in history, on the cross, but again and again? Today. Now.
>
> It's at times like this that we have to remind ourselves of the very core of the Christian faith. There are other worlds than this. This world, that seems so real, is no more than a shadow of the life to come. If we believe that all is well in this present life, if we can imagine nothing more satisfactory than this present life, then we are under a dangerous illusion. All is not well. Believe me, all is not well.
>
> (*His present experience, Joy's suffering, breaks through the familiar pattern of his lecture.*)
>
> Suffering…by suffering…through suffering, we release our hold on the toys of this world, and know that our true good lies in another world.
>
> But after we have suffered so much, must we still suffer more? And more?[6]

Lewis is tormented by this question to which he has no

answer. He can only repeat familiar lines about God making us perfect through suffering. He desperately wants to believe that to be true.

What makes Lewis so attractive in this scene is that a part of us identifies with his torment. The redemptive meaning of suffering encourages the religious believer in bearing suffering, even if it is still difficult.

The virtue of hope does not glorify suffering and death, nor does death cease to be death. But hope does give us a way to approach suffering and death without being overcome with despairing meaninglessness that turns to mercy killing as a way to manage dying. God's love, revealed in the resurrection of Jesus, gives the courage and the hope to enter into suffering and death knowing that life ultimately triumphs. If, through suffering, Lewis and Joy are brought nearer to God in Christ, then they may bear it courageously because of the comfort of the spiritual experience it offers. The bonding with Christ is the means for managing suffering and dying well.

These are but three virtues which give us strength of character and a spiritual vision which enable us to live well while dying, even in the face of those conditions of hopelessness which threaten to overwhelm us. But we cannot acquire these virtues nor die a peaceful death if we are not already nurtured by a community of virtue. In addition to personal virtue, we also need to be a community which gives witness to those fundamental religious and moral convictions which shape our living and our dying in ways that would make euthanasia unthinkable.

THE VIRTUOUS PARISH

We look to our parishes to provide not only resources for service but also to be resources for meaning, support, and identity in a culture that is antagonistic in so many ways to gospel vision and values. The parish is uniquely positioned to witness to the meaning of life formed in the light of the gospel and to be a resource of support for those who live in the light of faith. It is there for all ages and socioeconomic groups. It ministers to all stages of life. It has structures for education, it invites volunteers, and it offers opportunities for getting involved in the larger community. Three virtues stand out to characterize the parish as a healing place, where reassurance and hope, support and concern are brought together for its members.

A Community of Care

The liberating and life-giving power of a parish community is released by caring for one another, a virtue which enables us to enter Uncle Harry's life and, through empathy, to help make life worth living, even in the face of suffering. Stanley Hauerwas has it exactly right when he says that Christians have no "solution" to the evil of suffering. "Rather, they have had a community of care that has made it possible for them to absorb the destructive terror of evil that constantly threatens to destroy all human relations."[7] Our parishes are uniquely situated to be this community of care that surrounds the sick and dying with support.

In the high-tech, low-touch world of modern medicine, skilled technical interventions have pushed aside the practice of keeping compassionate company with patients. Instead, caring appears as the consolation prize when science and technology do not win. The public interest in euthanasia has drawn attention to the limits of modern medicine to cure and to assure a peaceful death. True caring includes curing when possible, but it also accepts decline and death as part of being human. True caring also entails persistent presence, careful listening, and a willingness to enter deeply into Aunt Sally's suffering, our neighbor Marilyn's, and even the stranger Stan's in order to help absorb the terror and share the burden a seriously ill person feels. A caring community can help the sick and dying bear burdens which come as part of the limitation of being human.

A moving story about bearing burdens was told during the days when California was debating Proposition 161, the Death with Dignity Act. The story was about Bob, a gay man, and his partner Ian's assisted suicide. Ian had AIDS but no health insurance to pay his medical bills. Bob sold some of their shared art pieces to get more money to pay bills. When Ian realized that the art work which they loved was gone, he knew what Bob was up to. Ian felt like an albatross around Bob's neck. But Ian was not about to let Bob ruin himself and all that Bob had worked for just to give Ian another week or more to live. Bob loved Ian and went back and forth on whether Proposition 161 would be good social policy. So Bob thought, "If euthanasia becomes legal, why not put Ian and all those suffering with AIDS out of their misery? They're going to die anyway." What Bob realized is that those suffering like Ian who supported euthanasia wanted to put themselves out of what they thought was misery for their care-givers. But Bob captured the heart of the matter when he said, "I'd endure anything, give all I have, to have Ian back for just one day. It still hurts me that he didn't understand that." This story raises so clearly the question, "Whose burdens are we really relieving when we turn to euthanasia?"

The Catholic moral tradition offers some help to guide our actions when burdens become overwhelming. According to the tradition, no one is morally obliged to bear burdens beyond their capacity. Our tradition values life as a basic condition necessary to achieve all other values; but it does not demand an idolatrous reverence that makes physical life an absolute value to be sustained at all costs. It is not a license to kill. The wisdom enshrined in the traditional ordinary/extraordinary distinction is that when burdens become overwhelming, then we can withhold or withdraw further treatment and allow the natural progression of the disease to run its course. A caring community can help Mom accept the limits of being human and say, "Stop! Enough is enough."

When we stop our medical interventions because they can no longer lighten the burdens and bring reasonable relief of suffering, the moral obligation turns to intensify efforts of caring that ease the burden of dying. Hospice workers frequently report that when they direct their resources to alleviating pain and discomfort, as well as attending to spiritual, emotional, and financial concerns, requests for assistance in dying are extremely rare. Intensifying efforts to care is the responsible way to face the limits of mortality and of medical power with an attitude that does not despair. Then caring is not the consolation prize for an unattainable cure, but is integral to the style and plan of treating the whole person.

Furthermore, a caring community also encourages us to face the limits of mortality before the critical moment of imminent death when we confront those hard choices of whether to treat or not to treat. There is a bumper sticker that reads, "Life's a bitch, and then you die." Given the dependency, pain, and disability most fear before dying, the sticker seems too optimistic. Perhaps the more common sentiment might be the pessimistic one, "Life's a bitch, *you linger*, and then you die." The fear of lingering in unacceptable conditions of dependency and disability brought about by medicine's power to prolong dying encourages support for euthanasia.[8]

Perhaps we would not have to consider euthanasia a possible option if more people knew that they could set limits on their own treatment. Encouraging conversations about limits with one's physician and family members is one way to do this. Another is through the use of legal documents of advance directives. Parishes which are to be centers of healing can encourage the use of these documents and make them available in their pamphlet racks. The Catholic Health Association[9] provides model documents that are in line with the Catholic moral tradition on the proper care of the dying.

A community of care might also promote more preaching about facing limits, living with mortality, suffering and death. Waiting until a funeral to address such issues is too late. That is not the best time that people can absorb the Christian message on these themes. Other liturgical times offer better opportunities, especially a communal anointing of the sick and the season of Lent, which are partly focused around the theme of suffering. Without a spiritual vision, we risk encouraging merely technical ("curing") solutions to the inevitability of aging, sickness, suffering and death. When that happens, we lose sight of human wholeness as the goal of care not only in the middle of life but also at its end.

Caring communities also can provide educational services to help people stay well, cope with stress, and learn to face death. Educational programs on death and dying that include representatives of religion, medicine, and psychology are another way to provide care for the well-being of the parish community. For example, St. Peter's school experienced the death of two students, one from leukemia and the other from an automobile accident. The school responded by offering a course on death and dying by an interdisciplinary team of the school counselor, the parish priest, and a hospice nurse. The success of the course gave rise to a similar program offered for adult enrichment on Sunday mornings.

Moreover, the church is the place where we would expect to bring faith and health together. More people are beginning to realize that life is holistic, and they want to include their faith and spirituality in that outlook. What better place to promote holistic faith and spirituality than the church, where the emphasis is on building inner resources for strength and health? The time is right to capitalize on the growing popular interest in fitness, good health habits, and creative ways to manage stress. Parish halls and schools can provide Holistic Health Centers with periodic "health fairs" which make available various programs that focus on managing health in morally responsible ways. There is no limit to the church's contribution to preventive medicine and to shaping the outlooks of everyone who wants to know how faith informs living, suffering, and dying.

A Community of Hospitality

Becoming a community of care is activated by being a community of hospitality. The Second Vatican Council highlighted this characteristic by describing the church, and life itself, as a pilgrimage. As fellow travelers, or pilgrims, on the journey through life, we need a place of hospitality.

One way this hospitality is being provided to the dying is through hospice care. "Hospice," a term derived from the Latin for "hospitality," originally meant a lodging for travelers. Today, instead of being a particular place, hospice is a concept of care that satisfies many of the requirements for the virtue of hospitality. For example, hospice care respects Aunt Rose in a holistic way, it improves the conditions of her dying by being aggressive with managing pain, and it reaches beyond Aunt Rose's needs for comfort to her network of support by providing relief for caregivers and, if needed, grief counseling for survivors after she dies. Home hospice, however, still serves too few terminally ill patients. It is time to encourage keeping more of the dying at home where they can be surrounded by familiar people, sights, sounds, and smells.

A parish community can be hospitable in the way it provides for people who can visit and communicate to the sick, the shut-ins, and the dying to show them that they are worthy of respect, that their lives have meaning, and that they are not being isolated or abandoned. Suffering, in chronic illness or as life ends, is exacerbated for those who are unable to form and sustain relationships of meaning and value. The loss of contact with others in any meaningful way spawns hopelessness and despair. Is it not true that when we find ourselves in contact with others, and when that communion is supported and nurtured, suffering is shared and thereby diminished, hope returns, and despair gives way to trust? Too often the fear of isolation is only reinforced when we respond with empty gestures or saccharine statements of reassurance. Everyone who has any contact with the sick, shut-ins, and the dying needs to be more conspicuously visible and to keep company with them more often, to talk about what is important to them and to listen to their needs, fears, questions, and hopes. This responsibility to be present to the suffering must not be relegated to only a few. As The Rite for the Pastoral Care of the Sick reminds us,

> This ministry is the common responsibility of all Christians, who should visit the sick, remember them in prayer, and celebrate the sacraments with them. The family and friends of the sick, doctors and others who care for them, and priests with pastoral responsibilities have a particular share in this ministry of comfort. (Intro., no. 43)

But to be hospitable in this way demands giving up what so many of us have so little of—time. Hospitality does not ask for a lot of time, but enough so that the sick and dying feel accepted and know that they enjoy a respectful place in our lives.

A parish community of faith can support relationships of

meaning and value and amplify them through religious symbols, rituals, and stories. Take sharing stories, for example. The hospitable community that takes the time to listen to the sick and dying tell their stories is providing them with a way to acknowledge that their lives have made a difference. To mean something to someone else or to know that you are deeply cared for is reason itself for living. The hospitable community which in turn shares stories of faith can enable the suffering to see how their lives reflect God's story and witness to the transforming power of God. Connecting through stories may not relieve all the anxiety that the sick and dying may feel, but it may help them to connect their suffering to that of Jesus and so affect their outlook toward their suffering.

Resources of prayer and ritual, especially the thoughtful celebration of the sacraments, are also extremely important to people facing death. In the Catholic tradition, we believe that prayer makes explicit and personal the community's relationship to the dying person. To this end, many parishes rightly follow the practice of remembering the sick and dying in the General Intercessions at the Sunday mass. This helps to keep the whole community connected to them in faith and in love.

The Catholic tradition has also long affirmed that sacraments are a privileged moment of heightening an experience of God's love. The eucharist is at the heart of the church's life as an encounter with the risen Lord. The sacrament of reconciliation can restore harmony to the self and provide the sense of forgiveness needed to face the crisis of dying. The anointing of the sick reflects God's compassion and the community's care so that the sick will not lose faith or hope.

Another way the parish can be a hospitable community is in caring for the care-givers. The heart of the issue in responding to debilitating, chronic, and lingering illnesses is the human heart itself. How much can it take? The lack of supportive care for those who spend endless hours caring for the terminally ill has been a crucial factor in cases of euthanasia.[10]

In order to provide supportive care to the care-givers, some parishes have organized volunteer groups, such as the Martha Ministries or the Stephen Ministries. These may take the form of providing temporary relief from care-giving so that families can have some time off or look after personal or family business. It may also include providing some meals, doing shopping, laundry, or house cleaning. It may also involve advising them on how to get access to services which provide financial support.

Hospitality to care-givers also includes helping them emotionally and spiritually as they deal not only with Grandma's death, but with their own fear of death. One way of doing this is to give care-givers time to tell their own story of living with Grandma and to tell those parts of her story which she did not get a chance to tell. Hospitality also includes listening to the shock and anger which survivors still feel lest it overwhelm them and lead to depression and despair. Ongoing support groups for the bereaved, too, can be a helpful way to complete unfinished business and to heal what still needs to be mended.

A Community of Interdependece

To make our efforts to be caring and hospitable more efficient, and to make the Catholic moral vision credible, we need to share life interdependently. The challenge of today's parish in a culture infected with individualism is to help convert society from being a collection of individuals pursuing their own self-interests to becoming an interdependent community where all give and all receive. St. Paul's metaphor of the community as the body of Christ (1 Cor 12) can be our guiding image. Just as the body cannot be identified with any one of its parts, no part can take the place of any other. Each contributes to the whole.

One way the parish community can contribute to the bonding that can make living interdependently liberating and life-giving is by facilitating the collaboration of the various communities which make up the church. For example, in our church today, parishes, schools, hospitals, and religious organizations often operate independently of one another in order to protect their own self-interests. We suffer today not only from personal individualism but also from communal individualism. A challenge for today's parish is to get all these communities to collaborate as partners in the larger ministry of serving the health of its members.

To achieve effective collaboration demands a center of coordinated efforts. To this end, parishes might well institute a health ministries program, or what some call a parish nurse program,[11] to coordinate health care services within the parish community. Religious-sponsored hospitals are finding these programs compatible with their mission, and cooperation, in principle, should be easy. Furthermore, in these days of health care reform, such a collaborative partnership can be a creative way to show responsible stewardship of our resources.

The role of the parish nurse is to find ways of responding to the health concerns of the parish, but not personally to care for the ill in the parish. The parish nurse is in a unique position to help parishioners understand the relation of faith and health, to access community resources, and to better manage their physical, emotional, and spiritual health. A job description of a parish nurse would include such tasks as educator and coordinator of programs that promote wellness; forming and facilitating support group activities responding to life situations such as cancer, AIDS, chronic illness, divorce, and prayer requests; providing home and institutional visitation programs; providing preventive and primary health care for blood pressure and cholesterol screening, child immunization programs, and the like; and providing assistance to understand and access the local health care system. At this critical time in health care, the parish nurse program can offer both the parish and the hospital an opportunity to witness to the power of communal interdependence that serves the good of all.

CONCLUSION

That we all will have to face experiences of pain, suffering, and death in ourselves and in others is the price of being human. While this fact is biologically determined, there is nothing fixed about how we will respond to it. What sickness and the threat of death do to us is one thing. What we make of them is another. The way we respond is a matter of character being shaped over the course of our lives, and not just in the time of crisis.

People are responding differently to the euthanasia movement because they have different ideas about who we ought to be, where to find meaning in life, how much control we ought to have, what to make of suffering, and what we owe to one another. This chapter of a pastoral response has explored some of these issues through the lens of virtue, personal and corporate. These are the virtues we might want to nurture if we are going to rise to the occasion and alleviate those conditions of hopelessness which can make euthanasia so attractive. Only if we can rise to the occasion with compelling witness to our religious convictions about life, suffering, and death will we ever have an impact on shaping public consensus toward death as an experience that we need not hasten through lethal interventions.

CONCLUSION

Positioning the debate on euthanasia within the framework of the scope of autonomy, the prohibition of killing, and beneficence can too easily suggest that the euthanasia debate ultimately turns on moral arguments. It does not. The debate is fundamentally about the nature and meaning of human life. As such, it calls for a spiritual vision and moral conversion more than for moral arguments.

In the end, the Catholic position on euthanasia ultimately rests on the kind of community we become. Our convictions about sovereignty, stewardship, sanctity of life, suffering, and mercy call us to witness to the powerlessness that comes with the limits of human control over life and death. It also comes by responding to the conditions of hopelessness which make euthanasia so attractive. Responding to the fears of losing control, meaning, and company by becoming a caring community will be a witness to the hope that, although life may be hard, it can still be lived. Supporting euthanasia would be a rejection of the abiding presence of God manifest in the covenantal commitments of being a community committed to caring mercifully for those who cannot be cured.

APPENDIX:
DECLARATION ON
EUTHANASIA

Vatican Congregation for the Doctrine of the Faith
June 26, 1980

Introduction

The rights and values pertaining to the human person
occupy an important place among the questions discussed
today. In this regard, the Second Vatican Ecumenical Council
solemnly reaffirmed the lofty dignity of the human person,
and in a special way his or her right to life. The council therefore condemned crimes against life "such as any type of
murder, genocide, abortion, euthanasia, or willful suicide"
(Pastoral Constitution "Gaudium et Spes," no. 27).

More recently, the Sacred Congregation for the Doctrine of
the Faith has reminded all the faithful of Catholic teaching
on procured abortion. The congregation now considers it
opportune to set forth the church's teaching on euthanasia.

It is indeed true that, in this sphere of teaching, the
recent popes have explained the principles, and these
retain their full force; but the progress of medical science in
recent years has brought to the fore new aspects of the

question of euthanasia, and these aspects call for further elucidation on the ethical level.

In modern society, in which even the fundamental values of human life are often called into question, cultural change exercises an influence upon the way of looking at suffering and death; moreover, medicine has increased its capacity to cure and to prolong life in particular circumstances, which sometimes give rise to moral problems.

Thus people living in this situation experience no little anxiety about the meaning of advanced old age and death. They also begin to wonder whether they have the right to obtain for themselves or their fellowmen an "easy death," which would shorten suffering and which seems to them more in harmony with human dignity.

A number of episcopal conferences have raised questions on this subject with the Sacred Congregation for the Doctrine of the Faith. The congregation, having sought the opinion of experts on the various aspects of euthanasia, now wishes to respond to the bishops' questions with the present Declaration, in order to help them to give correct teaching to the faithful entrusted to their care, and to offer them elements for reflection that they can present to the civil authorities with regard to this very serious matter.

The considerations set forth in the present document concern in the first place all those who place their faith and hope in Christ, who, through his life, death and resurrection, has given a new meaning to existence and especially to the death of the Christian, as St. Paul says: "If we live, we live to the Lord, and if we die, we die to the Lord" (Rom 14:8; cf. Phil 1:20).

As for those who profess other religions, many will agree with us that faith in God the Creator, Provider and Lord of life—if they share this belief—confers a lofty dignity upon every human person and guarantees respect for him or her.

It is hoped that this Declaration will meet with the approval of many people of good will who, philosophical or ideological differences notwithstanding, have nevertheless a lively awareness of the heights of the human person. These rights have often in fact been proclaimed in recent years through declarations issued by international congresses; and since it is a question here of fundamental rights inherent in every human person, it is obviously wrong to have recourse to arguments from political pluralism or religious freedom in order to deny the universal value of those rights.

I. The Value of Human Life

Human life is the basis of all goods, and is the necessary source and condition of every human activity and of all society. Most people regard life as something sacred and hold that no one may dispose of it at will, but believers see in life something greater, namely a gift of God's love, which they are called upon to preserve and make fruitful. And it is this latter consideration that gives rise to the following consequences:

1. No one can make an attempt on the life of an innocent person without opposing God's love for that person, without violating a fundamental right, and therefore without committing a crime of the utmost gravity.
2. Everyone has the duty to lead his or her life in accordance with God's plan. That life is entrusted to the individual as a good that must bear fruit already here on earth, but that finds its full perfection only in eternal life.
3. Intentionally causing one's own death, or suicide, is therefore equally as wrong as murder; such an action on the part of a person is to be considered as a rejection

of God's sovereignty and loving plan. Furthermore, suicide is also often a refusal of love for self, the denial of the natural instinct to live, a flight from the duties of justice and charity owed to one's neighbor, to various communities or to the whole of society—although, as is generally recognized, at times there are psychological factors present that can diminish responsibility or even completely remove it.

However, one must clearly distinguish suicide from that sacrifice of one's life whereby for a higher cause, such as God's glory, the salvation of souls or the service of one's brethren, a person offers his or her own life or puts it in danger (cf. Jn 15:14).

II. Euthanasia

In order that the question of euthanasia can be properly dealt with, it is first necessary to define the word used.

Etymologically speaking, in ancient times euthanasia meant an easy death without severe suffering. Today one no longer thinks of this original meaning of the word, but rather of some intervention of medicine whereby the sufferings of sickness or of the final agony are reduced, sometimes also with the danger of suppressing life prematurely. Ultimately, the word euthanasia is used in a more particular sense to mean "mercy killing," for the purpose of putting an end to extreme suffering, or saving abnormal babies, the mentally ill or the incurably sick from the prolongation, perhaps for many years, of a miserable life, which could impose too heavy a burden on their families or on society.

It is therefore necessary to state clearly in what sense the word is used in the present document.

By euthanasia is understood an action or an omission which of itself or by intention causes death, in order that all suffering may in this way be eliminated. Euthanasia's terms of reference, therefore, are to be found in the intention of the will and in the methods used.

It is necessary to state firmly once more that nothing and no one can in any way permit the killing of an innocent human being, whether a fetus or an embryo, an infant or an adult, an old person, or one suffering from an incurable disease, or a person who is dying. Furthermore, no one is permitted to ask for this act of killing, either for himself or herself or for another person entrusted to his or her care, nor can he or she consent to it, either explicitly or implicitly. Nor can any authority legitimately recommend or permit such an action. For it is a question of the violation of the divine law, an offense against the dignity of the human person, a crime against life, and an attack on humanity.

It may happen that, by reason of prolonged and barely tolerable pain, for deeply personal or other reasons, people may be led to believe that they can legitimately ask for death or obtain it for others. Although in these cases the guilt of the individual may be reduced or completely absent, nevertheless the error of judgement into which the conscience falls, perhaps in good faith, does not change the nature of this act of killing, which will always be in itself something to be rejected.

The pleas of gravely ill people who sometimes ask for death are not to be understood as implying a true desire for euthanasia; in fact it is almost always a case of an anguished plea for help and love. What a sick person needs, besides medical care, is love, the human and supernatural warmth with which the sick person can and ought to be surrounded by all those close to him or her, parents and children, doctors and nurses.

III. The Meaning of Suffering for Christians and the Use of Painkillers

Death does not always come in dramatic circumstances after barely tolerable sufferings. Nor do we have to think only of extreme cases. Numerous testimonies which confirm one another lead one to the conclusion that nature itself has made provision to render more bearable at the moment of death separations that would be terribly painful to a person in full health. Hence it is that a prolonged illness, advanced old age, or a state of loneliness or neglect can bring about psychological conditions that facilitate the acceptance of death.

Nevertheless the fact remains that death, often preceded or accompanied by severe and prolonged suffering, is something which naturally causes people anguish.

Physical suffering is certainly an unavoidable element of the human condition; on the biological level, it constitutes a warning of which no one denies the usefulness; but, since it affects the human psychological makeup, it often exceeds its own biological usefulness and so can become so severe as to cause the desire to remove it at any cost.

According to Christian teaching, however, suffering especially suffering during the last moments of life, has a special place in God's saving plan; it is in fact a sharing in Christ's passion and a union with the redeeming sacrifice which he offered in obedience to the Father's will. Therefore one must not be surprised if some Christians prefer to moderate their use of painkillers, in order to accept voluntarily at least a part of their sufferings and thus associate themselves in a conscious way with the sufferings of Christ crucified (cf. Mt 27:34).

Nevertheless it would be imprudent to impose an heroic way of acting as a general rule. On the contrary, human and Christian prudence suggests for the majority of sick people the use of medicines capable of alleviating or suppressing pain, even though these may cause as a secondary effect semi-consciousness and reduced lucidity. As for those who are not in a state to express themselves, one can reasonably presume that they wish to take these painkillers, and have them administered according to the doctor's advice.

But the intensive use of painkillers is not without difficulties, because the phenomenon of habituation generally makes it necessary to increase their dosage in order to maintain their efficacy. At this point it is fitting to recall a declaration by Pius XII, which retains its full force, in answer to a group of doctors who had put the question: "Is the suppression of pain and consciousness by the use of narcotics permitted by religion and morality to the doctor and the patient (even at the approach of death and if one foresees that the use of narcotics will shorten life)?"

The Pope said: "If no other means exist, and if, in the given circumstances, this does not prevent the carrying out of other religious and moral duties: Yes." In this case, of course, death is in no way intended or sought, even if the risk of it is reasonably taken; the intention is simply to relieve pain effectively, using for this purpose painkillers available to medicine.

However, painkillers that cause unconsciousness need special consideration. For a person not only has to be able to satisfy his or her moral duties and family obligations; he or she also has to prepare himself or herself with full consciousness for meeting Christ. Thus Pius XII warns: "It is not right to deprive the dying person of consciousness without a serious reason."

IV. Due Proportion in the Use of Remedies

Today it is very important to protect, at the moment of death, both the dignity of the human person and the

Christian concept of life against a technological attitude that threatens to become an abuse. Thus, some people speak of a "right to die," which is an expression that does not mean the right to procure death either by one's own hand or by means of someone else, as one pleases, but rather the right to die peacefully with human and Christian dignity. From this point of view, the use of therapeutic means can sometimes pose problems.

In numerous cases, the complexity of the situation can be such as to cause doubts about the way ethical principles should be applied. In the final analysis, it pertains to the conscience either of the sick person, or of those qualified to speak in the sick person's name, or of the doctors, to decide, in the light of moral obligations and of the various aspects of the case.

Everyone has the duty to care for his or her own health or to seek such care from others. Those whose task it is to care for the sick must do so conscientiously and administer the remedies that seem necessary or useful.

However, is it necessary in all circumstances to have recourse to all possible remedies?

In the past, moralists replied that one is never obliged to use "extraordinary" means. This reply, which as a principle still holds good, is perhaps less clear today, by reason of the imprecision of the term and the rapid progress made in the treatment of sickness. Thus some people prefer to speak of "proportionate" and "disproportionate" means.

In any case, it will be possible to make a correct judgment as to the means by studying the type of treatment to be used, its degree of complexity or risk, its cost and the possibilities of using it, and comparing these elements with the result that can be expected, taking into account the state of the sick person and his or her physical and moral resources.

In order to facilitate the application of these general principles, the following clarifications can be added:

— If there are no other sufficient remedies, it is permitted, with the patient's consent, to have recourse to the means provided the most advanced medical techniques, even if these means are still at the experimental stage and are not without a certain risk. By accepting them, the patient can even show generosity in the service of humanity.

— It is also permitted, with the patient's consent, to interrupt these means, where the results fall short of expectations. But for such a decision to be made, account will have to be taken of the reasonable wishes of the patient's family, as also of the advice of the doctors who are specially competent in the matter. The latter may in particular judge that the investment in instruments and personnel is disproportionate to the results foreseen; they may also judge that the techniques applied impose on the patient strain or suffering out of proportion with the benefits which he or she may gain from such techniques.

— It is also permissible to make do with the normal means that medicine can offer. Therefore one cannot impose on anyone the obligation to have recourse to a technique which is already in use but which carries a risk or is burdensome. Such a refusal is not the equivalent of suicide; on the contrary, it should be considered as an acceptance of the human condition, or a wish to avoid the application of a medical procedure disproportionate to the results that can be expected, or a desire not to impose excessive expense on the family or the community.

— When inevitable death is imminent in spite of the means used, it is permitted in conscience to take the decision to refuse forms of treatment that would only secure a precarious and burdensome prolongation of life, so long as the normal care due to the sick person in similar cases is not interrupted. In such circumstances the doctor has no reason to reproach himself with failing to help the person in danger.

Conclusion

The norms contained in the present Declaration are inspired by a profound desire to serve people in accordance with the plan of the Creator. Life is a gift of God, and on the other hand death is unavoidable; it is necessary therefore that we, without in any way hastening the hour of death, should be able to accept it with full responsibility and dignity. It is true that death marks the end of our earthly existence, but at the same time it opens the door to immortal life. Therefore all must prepare themselves for this event in the light of human values, and Christians even more so in the light of faith.

As for those who work in the medical profession, they ought to neglect no means of making all their skill available to the sick and the dying; but they should also remember how much more necessary it is to provide them with the comfort of boundless kindness and heartfelt charity. Such service to people is also service to Christ the Lord, who said: "As you did it to one of the least of these my brethren, you did it to me" (Mt 25:40).

At the audience granted to the undersigned prefect, His Holiness Pope John Paul II approved this Declaration, adopted at the ordinary meeting of the Sacred Congregation for the Doctrine of the Faith, and ordered its publication.

Rome, the Sacred Congregation for the Doctrine of the Faith, 5 May 1980.

Franjo Card. Seper
Prefect
Jerome Hamer, O.P.
Tit. Archbishop of Lorium, Secretary

NOTES

Introduction

[1] Andrew Greeley, "Live and Let Die: Changing Attitudes," *The Christian Century* 108 (December 4, 1991):1124–1125.

[2] St. Louis: The Catholic Health Association, 1994.

[3] St. Louis: The Catholic Health Association, 1993.

The Debate

[1] Richard A. McCormick, "Physician-Assisted Suicide: Flight from Compassion," *The Christian Century* 108 (December 4, 1991): 1134.

[2] Corrine Bayley, "What I Learned from Proposition 161 about Health Care and the Public," *Ethical Currents* (March 1993): 5.

Autonomy

[1] For a critical review of this concept, see Leon Kass, "Is There a Right to Die?" *Hastings Center Report* 23 (January–February, 1993): 34–43.

[2] H. Tristram Engelhardt, Jr., "Death by Free Choice: Modern Variations on an Antique Theme," in Baruch A. Brody, ed., *Suicide and Euthanasia* (Dordrecht: Kluwer Academic Publishers, 1989), pp. 264–265.

³ Derek Humphry, "The Case for Rational Suicide," *Euthanasia Review* 1 (Fall 1986): 172–175; Helga Kushe, "Voluntary Euthanasia and the Doctor," *Free Inquiry* 89 (Winter 1988): 17–19.

⁴ California Association of Catholic Hospitals, *CACH Networking* (Fall 1992): 1.

⁵ Greeley, "Live and Let Die: Changing Attitudes," *The Christian Century* 108 (December 4, 1991): 1125.

⁶ Washington Catholic Conference, "The Initiative 119 Campaign: Sharing Insights," *Executive Summary* (St. Louis: Catholic Health Association, 1991): 1.

⁷ Daniel Callahan, "Can We Return Death to Disease?" *Hastings Center Report* 19 (January–February, 1989): 4.

⁸ (New York: Ballantine Books, 1972), p. 150.

⁹ Richard J. Clifford and Roland E. Murphy, "Genesis," in Raymond E. Brown, Joseph A. Fitzmyer, and Roland E. Murphy, eds., *The New Jerome Biblical Commentary* (Englewood Cliffs: Prentice Hall, 1990), p. 12.

¹⁰ Bernard Haring, *Medical Ethics* (Notre Dame: Fides Publishers, 1973), p. 149.

¹¹ Charles Dougherty, "The Common Good, Terminal Illness, and Euthanasia," *Issues in Law and Medicine* 9 (1993): 151–166.

¹² *Ibid.*, p. 154.

¹³ *Ibid.*, p. 152.

¹⁴ Daniel Callahan, "When Self-Determination Runs Amok," *Hastings Center Report* 22 (March–April, 1992): 52–55.

The Prohibition Against Killing

[1] Rachels' most sustained argument for euthanasia and against the moral significance of the distinction between killing and allowing to die is in *The End of Life: Euthanasia and Morality* (New York: Oxford University Press, 1986), pp. 106–128.

[2] Paul Ramsey, *The Patient as Person* (New Haven: Yale University Press, 1970), p. 153; also, *Ethics at the Edges of Life* (New Haven: Yale University Press, 1978), pp. 146–148.

[3] Robert Veatch, *Death, Dying and the Biological Revolution*. Revised edition (New Haven: Yale University Press, 1989), pp. 61–73.

[4] *Ibid.*, p. 74.

[5] James F. Childress, "Love and Justice in Christian Biomedical Ethics," in Earl E. Shelp, ed., *Theology and Bioethics* (Boston: D. Reidel Publishing Company, 1985), p. 227.

[6] Edward Shils, "The Sanctity of Life," in Daniel H. Labby, ed., *Life or Death: Ethics and Options* (Seattle: University of Washington Press, 1968), p. 12.

[7] Raymond F. Collins, *Christian Morality: Biblical Foundations* (Notre Dame: University of Notre Dame Press, 1986), pp. 49–63.

[8] Advances in the scientific understanding of narcotics and the process of dying make us re-think the application of the principle of double effect in the case of using analgesics on some dying patients. This is evident in the CHA report on pain management which states that we may not need to apply the principle of double effect to managing pain. Current medical research is calling into question whether the use of pain-killers is really the cause of respiratory depression that accompanies the dying process. Quoting from the chair of the Wisconsin Cancer Pain Initiative, the report states:

Death from respiratory depression is exceedingly rare in patients with cancer who chronically receive opioid analgesics for pain. As a person nears death, there is deterioration in respiratory function. However, these respiratory changes should not be confused with the effects of the opioids.

In a footnote, the report continues:

Clinically significant respiratory depression rarely occurs in patients with severe cancer pain, even those taking large doses of morphine, because pain is a powerful antagonist to this effect of opioids. Furthermore, tolerance to the respiratory depressant effects of morphine develops rapidly. I know of no evidence that chronic ventilatory failure is either common or severe in patients with severe cancer pain who have been titrated to receive repeated large doses of morphine.

From June L. Dahl, private correspondence, and D. E. Joranson, in Kathleen M. Foley, ed., *Advances in Pain Research and Therapy*, Vol. 616 (New York City: Raven Press, 1990), as found in CHA Report, "Pain Management," *Health Progress* 74 (January–February, 1993): 37 and 40.

[9] Callahan, "Vital Distinctions, Mortal Questions," *Commonweal* 115 (July 15, 1988): 399–401. His argument is repeated in "Can We Return Death to Disease?" in "Mercy, Murder, & Morality: Perspectives on Euthanasia," *Hastings Center Report*, A Special Supplement 19 (January–February 1989): 5–6; *What Kind of Life* (New York: Simon and Schuster, 1990), pp. 221–249.

[10] Tom L. Beauchamp and James F. Childress, *Principles of Biomedical Ethics*, Second edition (New York: Oxford University Press, 1983), pp. 119–120. President's Commission, *Deciding to Forego Life-Sustaining Treatment* (Washington: U.S. Government Printing Office, 1983), p. 72.

Beneficence

[1] Timothy E. Quill, "Death and Dignity: A Case of Individualized Decision Making,"*New England Journal of Medicine* 324, no. 10 (March 7, 1991): 693.

[2] Albert R. Jonsen, "Beyond the Physicians' Reference—The Ethics of Active Euthanasia," *Western Journal of Medicine* 149 (August 1988): 196.

[3] Leon Kass, "Why Doctors Must Not Kill," *Commonweal* 118 (August 9, 1991): 474.

[4] Daniel Callahan, "When Self-Determination Runs Amok," *The Hastings Center Report* 22 (March-April, 1992): 55.

[5] *Ibid.*

[6] Eric J. Cassell, *The Nature of Suffering* (New York: Oxford University Press, 1991), pp. 30–47.

[7] For a brief treatment of the meaning and transformation of suffering, see *Care of the Dying: A Catholic Perspective* (St. Louis: Catholic Health Association, 1993), pp. 42–45.

[8] Pope John Paul II, *On the Christian Meaning of Suffering*, St. Paul Editions (Boston: Daughters of St. Paul, 1984), p. 30.

[9] On the biblical witness of mercy, see E. R. Achtemeier, "Mercy, Merciful; Compassion; Pity," *The Interpreters Dictionary of the Bible*, Vol. 3 (Nashville: Abingdon Press, 1962), pp. 352–354.

[10] Stanley Hauerwas with Richard Bondi, "Memory, Community, and Reasons for Living: Reflections on Suicide and Euthanasia," *Truthfulness and Tragedy* (Notre Dame: University of Notre Dame Press, 1977), pp. 101–115.

Pastoral Response

[1] Cited in William F. May, *The Patient's Ordeal* (Bloomington: Indiana University Press, 1991), p. 3.

[2] Callahan, *The Troubled Dream of Life*, p. 149.

[3] Viktor E. Frankl, *Man's Search for Meaning*, trans. Ilse Lasch (New York: Pocket Books, 1963), p. 104.

[4] M. Scott Peck, *Further Along the Road Less Traveled* (New York: Simon and Schuster, 1993), p. 50.

[5] (New York: W.W. Norton & Co., 1975).

[6] William Nicholson, *Shadowlands* (New York: Penguin Books, Inc., 1990), pp. 59–60.

[7] Stanley Hauerwas, *Naming the Silences: God, Medicine, and the Problem of Suffering* (Grand Rapids: Wm. B. Eerdmans, 1990), p. 53.

[8] Daniel Callahan, "Can We Return Death to Disease?" in "Mercy, Murder, and Morality: Perspectives on Euthanasia," *Hastings Center Report*, A Special Supplement 19 (January–February 1989): 4.

[9] Write to The Catholic Health Association, 4455 Woodson Road, St. Louis, MO 63134-3797.

[10] Derek Humphry and Ann Wickett, *The Right to Die* (New York: Harper and Row, 1986), p. 133.

[11] For more information on the parish nurse program, consult The Parish Nurse Resource Center, Lutheran General Health Care System, 1775 Dempster St., Park Ridge, IL 60068-9708; also, The Health Ministries Partnership, St. Joseph Health System, P.O. Box 14132, Orange, CA 92613-1532.